THE SOLIDARITY STRUGGLE

HOW PEOPLE OF COLOR SUCCEED AND FAIL AT SHOWING UP FOR EACH OTHER IN THE FIGHT FOR FREEDOM

EDITED BY MIA MCKENZIE

FOREWORD BY CECE MCDONALD

BGD PRESS, INC.

First published 2016

by BGD Press, Inc.

Oakland, CA

Copyright © 2016 by Mia McKenzie

ISBN: 978-0-9886286-5-6 (pbk.) / ISBN: 978-0-9886286-6-3 (ebook)

To my wife, who stands in solidarity with me
every day of our lives.

Contents

Foreword:
Real Fucking Talk
by CeCe McDonald

SOLIDARITY. Noun. Meaning: unity or agreement or action, especially among individuals with a common interest; mutual support within a group.

I've been doing my share of what it looks like to be operating in solidarity with others, and I know how I want that to be reciprocated for myself.

I've been a black trans woman since I could remember. Well, I might not have known that, but I have always known that I was not an "average" person. I wasn't allowed to be an average person because my femininity was too apparent and it was hard for me to pretend I was someone I wasn't. I knew who I was, but my family's Christian values and the internalized transphobia and fear of burning in hell sent me into a frenzy. I *was* in hell. But, luckily for me, I had friends who knew what it was like to want to escape the violent cycles of traditional values and be ourselves.

My best friend at the time was Staci. I can remember her towering over me like a beautiful palm tree, graceful and strong. She was the first person I told that I was "gay". She looked at me for a second and said, "Ok, you're still my best friend!" When I was being bullied, she'd beat them up for me. She was the voice I couldn't find within myself. She made me feel so loved. In a time when I felt so conflicted about everything in my life, I've never felt so loved and cared for from another person. She let me be me, the queer femme trans girl that I am. And instead of challenging who I was or my identities, she took time to know who I was. She secretly encouraged me to do the extra-curricular activities I wanted to do, like join the cheerleading team and the dance program, and even wear some very cute cutoffs that were one of the highlights of my transitioning. I began to dress more "feminine" and from there my life became a whirlwind. The bullying got worse, my family began to disown me, and I became very rebellious towards those who went against me. Which felt like the entire world. I just totally didn't give a fuck. But my friend Staci was there. Sharing secrets and each other's shoulders to cry on. She encouraged me to fight back against my oppressors, from the bullies to the madness inside of myself. I did and it made me stronger. And it was Staci who helped me get there. This is what solidarity looked like for me as a young black trans femme.

While I was in jail and in prison, a lot of the men—the cis men—who were in those units with me were more understanding of who I was and what I was going through than a lot of people outside jail and prison, which was weird to me because of the ways in which people in prisons and jails are depicted throughout the media. A lot of people are victims in prison. If you're a person who identifies as femme or trans, you're at a higher risk of danger but I don't think that was the case for me. I think in prison more people were uneducated about anything outside of cisheteronormative ideas. So for a person like me to come into those spaces and give a person an education about sexual orientation and the difference between gender identity and sexual orientation, it was really weird. For me, being in jail, I know that I'm gonna see majority people of color. Society will give you this idea that people of color are more homophobic or transphobic than white people. I don't feel like that's true, but those ideas are upheld by white supremacy anyway. We have to talk to our people about sexual orientation and gender identities.

I've gotten a lot of support and a lot of the people who were part of my support committee were POC. My family, my friends, people who I went to grammar school with, a lot of people who I didn't know, who were really happy to see me come out of that situation as a better person. In the media, they gave a lot of indications of white people being my supporters but there were *a lot* of people of color. Surprisingly, a lot of cishet Black and Latino men, who supported me and were glad to see I made it out of that situation, that I beat a racist, transphobic attack the way that I did. They protected me in some ways. I could have been jumped and injured by any of the white supremacist gangs in prison but they told me to watch out for certain people. They had my back. People were looking at support that was coming from outside but I had a lot of support that was inside, too.

Still, a lot of folks *aren't* showing up for trans queer black femmes. As of this writing, thirteen trans women have been murdered since January 1st, and I didn't see folks advocating for them like people were for their cis counterparts who've garnered media spotlight and countless social media posts. There was no uproar for the deaths of any of the trans women who've been murdered, even for Mya Hall, who was shot by NSA security—which would usually have people in an uproar. Black woman shot by NSA and nothing. There was no march, no outcry, no trending hashtag. Why was the life of this woman not as important as Mike Brown, Eric Garner, or Sandra Bland? When operating in solidarity, people need to understand that it's not a one-way street. I've always been taught to do unto others as you want done unto you. Real fucking talk.

Since my release, I've been doing the #BlackExcellence tour with my friend Joshua Allen, who is a trans/GNC person. I think that people believe cuz we all identify outside of a cishet spectrum that we all have the same perspective, that we all have the same ideas, that we all have the same cultural background, that we all speak the same language, things like that. Being on this tour has opened my eyes as a trans binary person on the importance of listening to the perspective of a person who identifies as no gender but themselves. That's a learning experience for me. Just because we're both "different" don't mean that I understand what they're thinking or feeling.

Being on this tour with Josh has really opened my eyes. It made me see things differently, especially with the HB2 bathroom laws. As a passing trans woman, who hasn't really had people question which bathroom I use, understanding the danger a non-passing trans person faces in those situations has opened my eyes. I think about that with my friend Josh. How can I support them? It's not my place to speak for them, but I can ask them what their issues are and ask them how they want me to operate in solidarity with them.

One of the things I've been talking about a lot lately is the anti-blackness in the POC community. The Islamophobia that can sometimes exist within the LGBTQIA community. We need to talk about those things. It's time for us to start breaking those cycles. We need to have real, sincere and true dialogue about these issues without people feeling like their opinions are being invalidated. A lot of times people can try to shut you down and tell you you're wrong and we're not accomplishing anything with that. It's easy for us to pretend like everything is okay, but it's not. Look at the recent Orlando Pulse massacre and how people went straight from homophobia to Islamophobia. We need to understand that these things are happening: pinkwashing, whitewashing, classism, sexism, racism, all of these isms that are existing in our communities. POC communities, the

LGBTQI community. We need to have a real, true dialogue. It starts with us being more open with each other.

How can I, as a black trans woman, support you and vice versa? What would be possible for people of color if we all showed solidarity with each other?

We could bring a drastic change to these white supremacist societal structures that have been put in place to make us fail, to make us lose, to make us perish, to make us fall short. We could talk about the ways in which, together, we could better our communities for each other. How we could make our neighborhoods safer. How we could make our education better. How we could end homelessness for our youth. How we could give stable employment that's an actual, livable wage. How we could make safe spaces for all people.

That's what solidarity would look like for me.

I'm so grateful to be part of this book. I really hope that people can take what is written in this book, what is being shared, to build solidarity and make all of our communities better.

CeCe McDonald is young and passionate transgender activist. She uses storytelling to articulate the personal and political implications of her time in prison and ways to heal.

Introduction

by Mia McKenzie

The first time I ever thought about "PoC solidarity" was in 2006. Having been born and raised in a Black community, having gone to college at a predominantly white institution, I'd never really seriously considered "non-white people" as a group. I understood anti-Black racism. I understood white supremacy. Socio-politically speaking, I didn't think a whole lot about non-Black people of color. That is, I did not consider them at all in relationship to Black struggle.

Then, in 2006, while living in Denver, a woman I'd picked up at Denver Pride invited me to a group hangout for "PoC". It was the first intentionally PoC gathering I can ever remember attending. Later, I remember saying to the woman who brought me, "What if people of color worked together? *Everything would change.*"

When I started BGD in 2011, as a platform for queer and trans people of color, I believed that PoC solidarity—particularly solidarity between oppressed racialized groups—was possible. I believed that with a lot of hard work, a lot of care, a lot of understanding, we could create solidarity, not just interpersonally, not just in small communities, but on a larger scale. I believed that a revolution, one in which radical people of color would come together in the fight for freedom for us all, was nigh.

Nearly five years later, I look back on my optimism with some amusement. From where I am now, it's funny to think how much of a believer I was then. Because five years of doing work to amplify the voices of QTPoC, five years and thousands of interactions with people of color from all walks of life, has all but erased the lovely notions I had of PoC solidarity.

One thing I didn't understand back in '06 is that anti-Blackness is not only present, but is prevalent, in every non-Black PoC community, and the incentives white supremacy offers non-Black people of color to uphold anti-Blackness are simply too enticing to reject. Non-Black people of color, when offered a choice between solidarity with Black people and more access to whiteness, choose the latter virtually every time.

Even in the process of putting together this book, I was subjected to anti-Blackness by non-Black people of color. Imagine having to reject a piece for a collection about PoC solidarity because the piece was too anti-Black. Now imagine having to do it multiple times.

There are other enormous barriers to building solidarity across racially oppressed groups, erasure of Indigenous peoples and xenophobia most prominent among them. When you add solidarity *within* racialized groups—solidarity with trans people of color, disabled people of color, fat people of color, incarcerated people of color—the list of barriers gets longer and longer.

Who are we talking about when we say "people of color"? In this book, we're mostly talking about Black and brown peoples in the western world, living in racialized bodies under white supremacy.

But wait. I know what you're probably thinking right now. If I don't believe that PoC solidarity is possible, why edit a book about it at all?

The simple answer is that, regardless of what I personally believe right now about our capacity to build solidarity across our differences, I still know that these are important conversations to have. One of my favorite lines from any work of literature is from Alice Walker's *Possessing the Secret of Joy* that proclaims: "Resistance is the secret of joy."

This I believe. I believe that these conversations, however difficult, are part of the ways we resist oppression and, therefore, part of the ways we find purpose and joy. Turning these questions over, hashing these problems out, is part of how we push back. And whether or not I believe in the possibility of solidarity, I believe, always, in pushing back.

The not-so-simple answer is that somewhere deep down I still do hope it's possible.

Remember when I said I'd been subjected to anti-Blackness even in the process of editing this book? Well, there's more to that story. There's my not-at-all-productive response to it. And there's Kelly Hayes.

Kelly is a queer Indigenous abolitionist based in Chicago. When I was near my wit's end in this process, sick of anti-Blackness and people's lack of accountability around it, asking myself (and my wife) if I should even continue, I reached out to Kelly for help. I didn't know her, I had only read her work about Black and Native solidarity, among other things, and found it comforting and brilliant. I asked if she'd be interested in writing a piece and/or editing one or two pieces for this collection. I told her what my intentions were for this project and, once she expressed interest, I told her everything. I told her about the most difficult parts of the process so far, namely anti-Blackness from Indigenous people and my reactions to it.

I let her know that I wasn't interested in pretending this isn't messy work for the sake of publishing this book, but rather that I wanted to take a step back, be accountable, and be intentional about how to improve the process and center the most crucial voices in this conversation—Indigenous people and Black people.

"So, for me that means first taking a step back and realizing that my many experiences of anti-Blackness from Indigenous people has affected the way that I show up in these interactions. I've pushed back against Indigenous people who, with no care or nuance whatsoever in regards to the brutal enslavement of my ancestors, call Black people "settlers," and have been accused of being anti-Indigenous because of it. I, frankly, come to the table now expecting anti-Blackness and, although it may be warranted, it makes it very difficult to build. What could simply be oversights on the part of a writer working on a first draft occurs in my body as anti-Black violence and I react, however subtly (or not), from that place. I'm unable to give folks the benefit of the doubt. Which, again, in whatever ways that might be understandable, doesn't make for good relationship building. I don't want to cause harm to other people of color; I don't want to continue these cycles of harm that we cause each other(...)

I'm(...)working on being able to both hold the reality that anti-blackness exists in Indigenous (and all other) communities AND being able to see individual writers through more than this painful lens. The key to this for me, I think, is in remaining open to feedback about how I may be being anti-Indigenous, prioritizing healing, and remembering what's at stake in this struggle."

I hit send and held my breath.

Kelly responded with understanding. "I know from my organizing here in Chicago that solidarity is always a messy matter," she wrote, "and that we are all constantly negotiating with various traumas. My direct action collective is exclusively Black and Brown, and we have a lot of conversations about how we, as Black and Brown femmes and non binary folx, succeed and fail in these matters. It's a lot, and it's definitely an ever evolving process for each of us. I am very excited to contribute to the project."

I cried, y'all. Because in the moment when I felt most exhausted over so-called "solidarity" and the way we constantly fucking fail at it, Kelly showed up. She wrote a piece and edited two pieces. More than that, she *saw me*. In a moment when I felt like most non-Black people of color could never really see me, no matter how much they pretended they could or wanted to. As corny as it may sound, I kept going with this book because I felt that as long as there are Kellys in the world, as long as there are people willing to do this messy fucking work, as long as there are folks who see your humanity and let you see theirs, there's hope.

So, that's why. Because I hope.

I hope because what I said to the woman I picked up at Denver Pride is true. Real solidarity between people of color *would* change everything.

This book is one tiny contribution to the conversation, one drop in the vast sea of successes and failures. It's not a comprehensive volume, it doesn't say everything that needs to be said—it couldn't possibly and that's not what it's meant to do. It's meant to help us turn some of these questions over, to help us hash some of these problems out, to help us push back.

There are tears in this book and there is anger. There is confusion and stumbling and trying again. There is sarcasm and resentment and heartache. And there is hope.

This book is meant to be a tool of resistance. And, through *resistance*, a tool of joy.

On Loving Each Other and Emptying Cages
How Black and Brown Power Will Set Us Free

by Kelly Hayes

Chicago police aren't really known for their restraint, but every once in awhile, they will attempt to negotiate a swift end to an act of civil disobedience, rather than commit to a mass arrest. As I lay on the cold asphalt at Congress Avenue and Clark Street, with my arms fixed into elaborately well-lit blockade devices, I knew that wasn't possible. Even as the police offered our organizers everything they could think of—no arrests for the blockade team, a clear path to Michigan Avenue, an unfettered march route down the Magnificent Mile for our supporters—we all knew it couldn't happen. Breaking the blockade, which had immediately brought at least two hundred cars to a screeching halt, was not an option, because, as our liaison cryptically explained to police, walking away from the action, free and clear, was "not the goal."

The police may have assumed that we were holding out because arrests would mean more media coverage. But with the spectacle of 16 blockaders in lockboxes, bearing a light for each homicide Chicago's racist policing hadn't prevented in 2015, we weren't particularly concerned about a lack of media attention. The goal that my friend Crystal couldn't actually spell out for police was that my collective, Lifted Voices, had announced on Twitter that our bail fund for this action had been tied to that of Naomi Freeman, a pregnant, Black abuse survivor who was trapped in Cook County Jail. The fundraising efforts for Naomi's bail had stalled and it seemed some drastic gestures would be necessary to bring her home for Christmas.

For our Black and Brown direct action collective, the struggle to free Naomi was a literal manifestation of everything we believe in.

Naomi took action in defense of herself, and her unborn child, which resulted in the death of her abuser. In a country where Black women are viewed, as Mariame Kaba has written, as having no selves to defend, the charges against Naomi were still more drastic than most would have imagined. She had been charged with first-degree murder for killing her longtime abuser, who had just subjected her to a near-fatal beating, and she was being held on $500,000 bail. A community of people who recognized the racism inherent in the charges against Naomi had rallied to bring her home, but needed further assistance.

Our collective, which centers the defense of Black and Brown femmes and non-binary people, was faced with a question of both will and creativity: How could we take this work we do, this action-oriented organizing that so often invokes words like "solidarity," to help empty a cage in real time? For us, it meant that some of us would have to put our bodies on the line and enter cages ourselves.

Image by Vicko Alvarez

Out of 16 blockade participants, many of whom were subjected to abuse and personal injury to break the blockade, most of our collective members who took arrest were Brown femmes. Indigenous members of our group, like myself, saw this moment as a crucial opportunity to not only help Naomi, but to lift up our belief that healing the wounds inflicted upon us by white supremacy—and the violence that white supremacy has led us to inflict upon each other—is what it's going to take for both Black and Brown communities to get free.

Since the onset of colonialism, white violence has pitted its Black and Brown targets against one another, and at times provoked our complicity. The Five Civilized Tribes—Indigenous nations that actually codified the ownership of Black people—enacted the violence of white supremacy on Black bodies at the behest of white society, just as the Black "Buffalo Soldiers" rode down Indigenous peoples, in support of westward expansion.

To understand where we are, and what we have yet to build, we must understand the violence of our shared histories. We cannot forgive what we cannot name, and our bitterness, grief and confusion, come from real places. We are traumatized, culturally, generationally and individually, and we often lack the patience that transformation demands.

It took me years, as a Native woman, to realize just how deeply anti-Blackness was embedded in our Brown communities, and how much I needed to interrogate my own reactions and ideas, at all times, to fight off the normative racism that this society smears into our consciousness. Lifted Voices, which merges Black and Brown power in action, has given that work a very tangible practice. Sharing a transformative framework that centers prison abolition, and a direct action curriculum that targets assumptions that make injustice seem inevitable, has given my pursuit of freedom new life.

But that night wasn't about my freedom, in any immediate sense. It was about compromising my liberty, for what would hopefully be a short time, so that a Black woman could give birth outside of a dungeon, and take joy in the smiles of her children on Christmas morning.

Regardless of how much one may fear police, electing to be jailed should inspire a certain level of reverence for the experiences of those who made no such choice. In workshops, Lifted Voices often compares sitting in jail, after an act of civil disobedience, to the experience of being in a hospital waiting room, in that one need not erase or deny their own emotions or experiences, but should always demonstrate a deep respect for what others are enduring. In the First District of Chicago's Police Department, that meant quietly watching a number of disheartened Black people move through the system, and hoping that their lives weren't being ruined forever. It's a cold, dark place, and some of us were treated pretty harshly, for a variety of reasons. But through it all, we knew that we were doing what we believe it takes to get free: merging our sense of solidarity, our love of community and our drive to take action in the streets.

From our youngest organizer's reassuring smile to our friend Delia's stoic reminders that every hour of our confinement was getting Naomi a little closer to free, I knew love in that dark place, and I even as I was harassed and intimidated, my imagination had never been so armed and ready. I could see freedom, not just for me, but for all of us, because I had just seen a group of Black and Brown femmes orchestrate a profoundly beautiful act of resistance that would also help empty a cage.

With groups like the Chicago Community Bond Fund, Love and Protect, Moms United Against Violence and Incarceration and the Women's Justice Fund, along with Naomi's family, fighting for every penny of Naomi's state-sanctioned ransom, our action helped carry their labor of love the last mile of the way. Naomi made it home for Christmas, and when we were sent a picture of her with her young children in front of a Christmas tree, nearly every member of our collective wept.

I won't describe what I was personally subjected to in jail, because this story isn't about me, but I will say that it was ugly, and that it was more than worth it. Because by showing up, living our values, and doing the work of resistance that we love so dearly, we helped a Black woman who the state saw as having no self worth defending.

Some time later, our entire collective—a dozen Black and Brown femmes and non-binary organizers—was invited to Naomi's baby shower. We went overboard on gifts and had prints made of the action, since we were told she had been moved by it. Experiencing the harshness of the state's violence, the cold air of a holding cell, the love of community and the joy of celebrating that a Black child would be born free, surrounded by all the beautiful people at that baby shower was the most complete experience of solidarity that I have ever known.

I am aware of my own people's struggles. Our water is toxic. Our children are taking their own lives at unthinkable rates. Our languages and lives are being stomped out by the state in the same historical rhythms of annihilation as they ever were. Really, the wars the United States has waged against Black and Brown peoples have changed little over time. While some still confuse access with ownership, many of us remain painfully aware that slavery, displacement and genocide have merely been refashioned over the course of these recent centuries. Law enforcement has clung to its origins, with police acting as slave catchers, to feed the prison industrial complex, and Indian Constables, enforcing the genocidal norms of white supremacy and colonialism.

And of course, today's efforts, such as those of Lifted Voices, are not newly conceived of. Our own militant approach to cultural, political and personal self defense is not an invention, but a tradition, following in the footsteps of the many Black and Brown revolutionaries who came before us. Our dreams of Black and Brown freedom fighters locking arms and tearing down both the walls that divide us and the empire that oppresses us, have been dreamt for generations. But this moment, this hope, these actions and this knowledge that our mutual struggle begins with showing up for each other, is ours to own and nurture. It is ours to meet with courage, patience and love, as we both strive and stumble. And we will stumble, as this is messy work, full of old wounds and emotional landmines. But when I stumble, and fall, and desperately need love, understanding, or even a fight waged in my name, I believe I'll be helped to my feet. Because I believe in the power we are all building together. I believe in our love of both Black and Brown people. And I believe that we will win.

Kelly Hayes *is a queer Indigenous direct action trainer and a co-founder of the direct action collective* Lifted Voices. *She is community relations associate and a contributing writer at* Truthout. *Kelly's analysis of state violence and movement work can also be found in the anthology,* Who Do You Serve, Who Do You Protect? *and the blog* Transformative Spaces.

I Interrupted the President To Stand Up For Trans Women in Detention Centers

by Jennicet Gutiérrez

President Barack Obama invited organizations, advocates, and leaders of the lesbian, gay, bisexual and transgender (LGBT) community to the White House in the summer of 2015 for an annual event called the Pride Reception. You could feel the excitement in the room as people were thrilled to be in the presence of the President—to hear him speak, to laugh at his jokes, and to take selfies with him. The event was intended to be a celebration of the achievements of the past year.

Although I believe in the importance of queer and trans people having access to marriage, this issue was not a priority for the undocumented transgender community. Undocumented trans women have no access to normative institutions such as marriage because they are facing detention and deportation.

I took full advantage of this moment to bring visibility to an issue many in our community would rather ignore: the deplorable conditions facing transgender women at the hands of Immigration Customs Enforcement (ICE), including torture and sexual and physical abuse. I did not become an activist to enjoy taking selfies with the President of the United States. I became an activist because of the daily violence, discrimination, and lack of opportunities impacting trans people.

At the same time the pride reception was taking place, trans murders in the US were on the rise. 2015 had the highest reported homicides against trans people, with the majority of the victims being black and Latina trans women. In addition to the transphobic and transmisogynist violence we face from institutions and individuals outside our communities, we experience another form of violence within our own communities, as the mainstream gay movement denies trans women solidarity, even as they've benefited from ours. Trans women have always been on the front lines, in particular during the Stonewall riot where Sylvia Rivera and Marsha P. Johnson were essential to the start of the movement for liberation.

One reason LGBT organizations deny us solidarity is because they do not see immigration as an LGBT issue and that both undocumented immigrants and trans women are not seen as human in our society.

When I was first approached about carrying out an act of civil disobedience during the Pride reception at the White House, I said yes without hesitation because of the urgency of this issue. It is an issue that became personal and political as I was undocumented at the time of the action and I am a brown transgender woman. Traveling to DC for the first time was thrilling as well as nerve-wracking. I did not have time to process what the outcome might be. I was concerned that because of my immigration status and criminal record, I was going to be denied access to this reception altogether.

Upon my arrival to DC, I met up with some activists who were looking forward to me being part of this event. I was extremely nervous and my body felt heavy. I had been unable to sleep the night before, waking up every few minutes, sweating and shaking. I hadn't been able to eat because I did not have an appetite. It was a humid day and we walked to the White House to get comfortable with the space and calm my nerves, and to visualize the action. Later, I tried get some rest.

The day of the action, I still felt tired, and nervous. I did not know if I was going to be able to deliver the message and speak on the conditions trans women face inside the detention centers. I was not sure if I was going to find the strength to speak truth to power. As I approached the first security checkpoint, I felt like my body was going to shut down. I felt like I was crossing the border for the second time. I cleared the first checkpoint. Then I cleared the second checkpoint, but I still didn't feel all there. I could not believe that I had gained access to the White House and was going to have an opportunity to actually challenge the LGBT community and the President on an issue they have intentionally ignored.

Then the moment came. The President came out and greeted the crowd. Many were smiling and taking selfies, most in attendance were ready to hear what the President might have to say about the imminent decision on same sex marriage. As I heard the words of the President, and the community cheering him on, I couldn't join the celebration because I kept thinking of the many challenges transgender women of color still face, even in a moment of progress.

Standing there with the President and leaders of the LGBT community, I found myself shaking and my heart was palpitating faster. When the President started to address the crowd, I was standing to the right, holding tight to my purse, remembering the demands, and thinking about the stories of Jessica and Nicole, trans women from Guatemala, who suffered physical and sexual abuse at the hands of ICE.

The moment I heard the President say how much progress we are making as a community was the moment I knew I had to raise my voice. That was the moment that I found the strength and spoke truth to power.

I demanded the release all LGBT people in detention centers and an end to the torture and abuse trans women face in detention centers.

My community had two options in that moment: to stand in solidarity with undocumented trans women or to turn their backs on us. Sadly, they chose the latter. I was shocked but not surprised. Two months prior to the interruption, I had watched a video where Sylvia Rivera took on a pride event in NYC in 1972 and spoke to the abuse her community was experiencing in the jails. She was also booed. She was also rejected.

LGBT leaders distanced themselves from standing in solidarity with me, and undocumented trans women in general, more concerned with their "progress" than with the lives and conditions of undocumented trans women. They sided with the President when he shut me down for challenging him, saying this was not the time or place. The leaders of the community booed me and said, "shhh, enough, this is not for you!"

But trans women of color rarely are given the platform to speak or make important decisions to improve our lives. I could not waste this opportunity.

It is of high importance to stand in solidarity with undocumented transgender women. If we can overcome our differences of opinion about how an action is delivered, if we can we can listen and give opportunities to speak and share our pain, we can move forward toward ending trans detention. We can stand in solidarity with the most marginalized in our community and put an end to torture and abuse. This is a moment to reflect. This is a moment to take a strong stance—a moral one— and stand with those of us who need support and solidarity.

Jennicet Gutiérrez *is a transgender organizer with* Familia: Trans Queer Liberation Movement. *She was born in Tuxpan, Jalisco, México. She believes in the importance of uplifting and centering the voices of trans women of color in all racial and trans justice work. Jennicet will continue to organize in order to end the deportation, incarceration and criminalization of immigrants and all people of color. She resides in Los Angeles.*

This is What White Supremacy Looks Like in Middle Class Black Communities

by Sydnee Thompson

When I was a kid, every time my family and I went into Detroit, there was a ritual we'd go through. We'd notice the gradual changes from suburban to urban: the cracked pavement, the weeds, the abandoned lots. I remember asking my mom why it was so easy to tell where one city stopped and the other one began, and why all the crumbling buildings were the ones Black people were living in.

So she told us what the city was like Before, when she was still there. There was nostalgia in her voice, and loss. I learned the history piecemeal: corrupt politicians, violent crime, poverty, etc., etc. There's nostalgia, but also distance. The story of the city is not our story—it's not my fate. After all, avoiding the despair of what happens there now is as easy as avoiding the exit ramp on the freeway.

But this distance is more than a coping mechanism: it's a disease, and suburbia is where it festers. Class divisions exacerbated by both geographical and metaphorical distance have helped make the metropolitan Detroit area one of the most segregated and racist in the country. Aiyana Jones, Renisha McBride, Terrance Kellom, and countless more, were all murdered just minutes from where I live.

White and Black still mix like oil and water, but about thirty years ago, Black people who could afford it started to push their way out. A trickle became a wave, and now the city that borders Detroit to the north, Southfield, is more than 70 percent middle class Black folk.

A lot, but not all, of us are the "good" ones, the respectable Blacks who are used by White people as bludgeons against the "bad" ones. I wish I could say that we're unwilling. Not quite.

There's the family member who sneered when I mentioned gentrification in the inner city—"who cares?" he said—and the friend who unironically quoted Chris Rock's infamous "I love Black people, but I hate niggers" routine to explain why he moved to the lily-est white suburb he could find. But it was when a Black associate I respected casually admitted to trashing job applications with names that sounded too ghetto that I wanted to scream.

These are the white lies my parents taught me: the ones they passed on out of a desperate need to feel safe under a white supremacist system. We didn't create them, but I still hear them roaring, like a powder keg about to blow.

***

My parents are a product of Detroit in the '60s and '70s. Born and raised there, they grew up on Motown, Belle Isle, and city buses. My grandmother marched with Dr. King when he previewed his "I Have a Dream" speech in Detroit; my parents were toddlers when he was assassinated. When the streets burned during one of the worst race riots in U.S. history, my grandparents looked on. And when the white people fled en masse, still unwilling to face the consequences of their racism, my family stayed and faced it in their place.

But to my parents, and many other Black people in the metro area, Detroit represents paradise lost: a Black majority city with leafy neighborhoods free of litter or crime. When the city couldn't promise that anymore (did it ever?), they packed their bags and never looked back. And in leaving behind our roots in the inner city, we were taught to demonize those who couldn't.

Respectability politics persists among Black people because it gives us the illusion of power. If you can escape the stifling conditions that a white supremacist, patriarchal society has destined for you—and maybe even flourish despite them—you can deny they exist. You can delude yourself into thinking that the bootstraps of white imperialists could ever be used to uplift the people they were meant to oppress.

But I didn't realize all of this until college, when I was taking classes at Wayne State University. It's smack dab in the middle of Detroit; disabled and coming of age in a recession, I wanted familiarity, and despite all its "problems," Detroit promised that.

It turned out to be familiar for the wrong reasons. In every honors class I took there, I was the only Black person...at a school that was twenty percent Black and a city that was over eighty percent Black.

In one of those whitewashed rooms, a professor lectured on white flight, gentrification, and race riots. He ripped the lid off of white supremacy and the lies it had infested metro Detroit's "best and brightest" with. There, I learned what it meant to be in a constant state of rage. In turn, my non-black classmates gave a presentation profiling a high achieving, majority black high school nearby. They tripped over their words, visibly struggling to explain why these "good" Blacks existed. Why I existed.

"We don't know why so many black kids struggle in school," one guy said instead. "Maybe they're just not as smart as other races."

My professor shut him down, but it was still wrong: he was also White.

Why was a White man (who thinks he'd be a Black person in another life) telling me what I should've known all along? Why was I at a university that proudly touted its love for Detroit but utterly failed at helping Black Detroiters succeed? And why didn't anyone seem to care?

When we throw the "bad" ones under the bus to get the scraps, what does it say about who and what is most important to us?

Detroit is a symbol of everything America hates—it's not

shocking that eventually, we'd come to hate it, too. But while I sat in those classrooms full of people who Didn't Get It and didn't want to, I realized I could no longer be one of them.

Being raised in the suburbs has given me access to resources that, thanks to a tax base gutted by persistent racism, Black people in poor and working class communities often don't have. As a Black person with class privilege, it's my responsibility to divest from respectability/meritocracy and redistribute those resources in any way I can. That means I support the fight for a living wage for all people, including our disabled family. When I want to devote my time, money, and knowledge to helping my communities, I will do so from a position of reciprocity, not domination, and I will always follow the lead of the people who have been doing the work from day one.

Our worth is not determined by our ability to codeswitch or by our zip code. I support my Black family in all the shades and shapes and hoods they come in, because I know they'd do the same for me. So for every White person or non-Black POC who might let their guard down around me and give me a seat at the table because I'm "safe," I want to make it my goal to prove they miscalculated. Being in solidarity with Black people with less socioeconomic privilege than me means I won't let the lure of personal success stop me from claiming my community or empowering it with tools white supremacist gatekeepers are determined to keep locked away.

Outside academia, in the real world, Detroit is supposedly

on the come up. White millennials are starting to move back to the city their parents destroyed. Thinkpieces abound featuring white saviors while even our conservative newspapers clumsily wonder where all the Black people are.

But we are here, even though the world still doesn't really see us. On a recent Friday night, I announced I was heading into the city to meet friends. "Don't get robbed," someone said. I felt that rage bubbling again, but I rolled my eyes and went about my business. I spent three plus hours at a table surrounded by unapologetic Black queer women, and it symbolized everything chasing respectability had stolen from me.

The cycle of white supremacy marches on. To the "good" ones: it doesn't need our help.

Sydnee Thompson is an editor, writer, and artist living in metro Detroit. They are passionate about creating, and advocating for, media that center nuanced but joyful experiences of marginalized people. They occasionally hang out on Twitter @SydMT.

Being in Solidarity with Me As a Transman & DV Survivor

by J Mase III

Writing this piece is painful for a lot of reasons. I have yet to meet anyone who enjoys talking about their trauma in public. I have yet to meet anyone who doesn't feel some sort of shame about the abuse they experienced. Furthermore, revisiting the disappointment you may have felt when you might have been let down, or were unable to get the help you needed to heal, is never a joyous moment. Yet, it is important, as we are able, to envision new possibilities. So, here I am.

A few years back, I was charged with leading discussions about domestic violence in the LGBTQ community as part of my non-profit job. I thought I knew something because someone called me an "expert". Someone who also had never experienced domestic violence. When I actually found myself in a violent relationship, I realized I knew nothing about DV, how to take care of myself, who to talk to and certainly not what to do once the relationship ended.

As a Black transman working at LGBTQ non-profits for a long time, I had all these different resources to refer clients to. As a survivor, it became clear to me just how many of those spaces did not have my specific challenges in mind. There are many things I wish folks knew about how to support me as a transman in a DV situation.

The domestic violence I experienced felt very gendered. As a transman who is not medically transitioning and is visibly gender non-conforming, I was dating a partner who had been on testosterone for years and often passed as a very masculine cis man. I felt I was being punished by my partner, through verbal assaults in public and private about my voice, appearance and desirability, for not being as passable. Out of the two of us, I also was the only person pulling in a living wage. In a world where my partner saw himself as ascending into his ideal manhood, me taking care of finances and other basic needs, and having the nerve to present as faggy as I did, seemed to make him resent me more. Here I was with another transman, feeling like my gender presentation made me a target.

Once my partner became physically/emotionally/financially abusive, it was expected that I could automatically close myself off to his humanity if it was really "that serious". However, abuse dynamics rarely start from the jump.

My partner didn't start out attacking me. He made arguments that sounded reasonable. Because some of the external factors that he was dealing with around money and family weren't getting better, his arguments got louder. His frustrations turned into insults I'm too ashamed to type. After that, it grew to throwing small objects. After that...well. It just progressed.

Abuse usually starts from a seemingly rational place. "Oh, he is looking for a job, that's why he is so testy today." "Oh, maybe I did do something that was insensitive to his needs." Successful relationships involve compromises. When someone starts to gaslight you, it becomes difficult to see the imbalance of those compromises.

It's hard, even in those moments, to not see the person attacking you as someone you care about who also needs help. I stayed because he was a human being who had some really amazing moments. Suddenly, I looked up and was in so deep I couldn't leave. He was dependent on me financially and because I worked from home often, it was hard to have space to even think about getting away.

Him being a Black transman, with a volatile temper, made me worried that going to the police would either have him in jail for the rest of his life or killed. I felt that since we shared this identity, it was my responsibility to protect him as best I could, even though he could have killed me.

I have had the unique blessing of being surrounded by a community of Black & Brown trans friends and colleagues. The reality when it comes to trauma is that the folks in your circle are the most likely to show up for you, but they are also the most likely to let you down. Unfortunately, many of the responses

I got from those from whom I sought support were also very gendered. People I knew to be very caring and quick when it came to femme- and women-identified folks going through assault and domestic violence were asking me, "Well, why didn't you fight him back?"

At one point a couple friends actually went to my abuser and told him what I had been saying. Not only did this put me in a situation to get physically assaulted more, but when I tried to address it with them later it was pushed off to the side through jokes and a lack of connection that they were now participating in the abuse. They even continued to work with him and request him for projects. I had trusted them because in a reverse situation, when one of those folks—who was woman-identified—was being targeted, we had all banded together to remove the abuser from our work and personal circles.

As survivors build up a safety plan that works for us (for me the police were not an option, gendered shelters were not an option) confidentiality is so key! When my ex started stalking me after the 3rd or 4th time he had broken up with me, I was scared to be in my home, to leave my home, and now folks in my community who never disputed what happened between the two of us were supporting him financially after putting my safety in danger. I often wondered if my confidence would have been kept had I not identified as a man. (Perhaps the expectation was that coming into real manhood meant you can't be open about assault?) The same folks I would see showing up against domestic and inter-community violence targeting my transfemme friends thought I just needed to toughen up. I was supposed to be physically stronger than, or at least as strong as, my abuser to stop it.

When I finally started being more open with people about what was happening, I was often asked what I needed. A handful of folks offered to support me by being accountability partners (think of this as a mediator between the victim of abuse and the abuser). Most of the folks who promised something did not follow through with what they offered. Having to re-tell your story again and again to folks forces you to relive the same trauma. I'd love to say I am fully healed or numb to the situation, but the reality was every day I told my story was another night I didn't sleep. To be waiting to hear from folks, to have to track them down, can put you back into the same feelings of worthlessness that you experienced being in that relationship. Here I was telling folks that I was scared for my life, and when folks didn't set realistic goals to be supportive, it felt like they didn't care about my life at all.

In the end, I moved 3000 miles away from my attacker because I felt like I didn't have enough people where I was living to keep me safe. Religious workers, social workers, healers in the same TQPOC community that was always teaching me about community accountability...told me to just move on. Even though the financial abuse that occurred was still impacting my daily life. Even though the PTSD kept me from working or seeing people or just breathing most of my day. People's ideal selves and actual selves are rarely in alignment. Many times they haven't even met yet. When we use words like accountability, when we create spaces that are in opposition to prisons, we must take seriously the need for alternative forms of justice. For me that was reaching out to accountability partners and, unfortunately, that didn't go anywhere. I didn't hate my ex. I was terrified and I wanted to hear from my community that I was worthy and that my pain was real.

No one is a better expert on what you need than you. I knew that to some degree before this experience. Being in solidarity with me as a survivor of violence as a Black trans man means deconstructing our gendered notions of violence. I can't tell you how many transmasculine folks have reached out to me in recent months to talk about their stories with partners, with sexual violence, and all with nowhere to go even though they are all linked to strong TQPOC communities. Most of the folks I reached out to for help were other Black trans people because that is the community I come from, love up on, and live for. We have so much healing to do, much of which goes unaddressed as we fight to survive all these different attacks on our bodies and spirits. I know why the folks I reached out to blamed me for being a victim of violence: many had to blame themselves to feel like they had control over their own lives and their abusers when it happened to them. How do we stop blaming ourselves for our trauma and create space to stop inflicting that pain on those who look like us?

J Mase III is a Black/trans/queer poet based in Seattle by way of NYC. He is the founder of awQward, the first trans & queer people of color specific talent agency. Check him out on Facebook, twitter and of course www.awQwardtalent.com!

Four Person-to-Person Things I Do to Address Anti-Blackness con Mi Gente

by CarmenLeah Ascencio

When my mothers married in 1989, I did not know that their union as a non-black Nuyorican and a black American was an anomaly for blacks and Latinxs in the U.S. I knew that their queerness was deviant, but not their black and brown love. I grew up thinking that black and brown love was innate, as I saw it in my family, my community and the history of unified black and brown liberation movements in the urban North East. It was not until I was older that I realized how much anti-blackness pervaded Latinx communities. At age 14 I discovered that anti-blackness was also inside of me, when I felt gratitude for being light skinned so I could be cast in more diverse theatrical roles. When I realized anti-blackness was within me, a girl who deeply loved her black mother, addressing anti-blackness became not only about justice and equality, but also about love and family.

The most recent anti-black state supported violence committed against Mike Brown, John Crawford, Ezell Ford, Eric Garner, Dante Parker and Marlene Pinnock prompted me to ask myself, how have I been accountable for addressing anti-blackness with my Latinx comunidad? Some powerful statements have been issued by Latinx organizations about anti-blackness among Latinxs and how to increase Latinx-Black solidarity. These articles have presented great large-scale ideas to change anti-black sentiment among Latinxs. *And*, if these systemic actions are not coupled with genuine relationships and solidarity on the ground, they don't have as much power. The Young Lords Party did not begin their struggle through changing policies or mainstream media. They challenged people in their community about anti-blackness and built a relationship with the Black Panther Party.

We Latinxs have got to do more to be in solidarity with our black familia, precisely because black people are OUR FAMILIA. If we don't start acting like black folks are our family in our personal interactions, white supremacy will gladly continue to divide and marginalize black and brown people through state-sanctioned violence. If we think we can make social change without addressing the anti-blackness that prevents the alliance of the 53 million Latinxs and 39 million black people in the U.S., we trippin'. So, here are four things that I do to address Latinx anti-blackness and move forward in la lucha with our black familia. I don't always get it right, but I'm clear it's my responsibility as a non-black Latinx to stay trying.

1. **I address anti-blackness when it comes up in my family and Latinx community.** We've all had the experience. You're sitting around enjoying the company of tu gente laughing and feeling some precious sense of belonging with your Latinx familia, when ¡PAO! – a friend or family member drops a line about those "negros". You feel a pit in your stomach. Quick! Do you say something and risk losing that momentary sense of belonging you so rarely get to feel in white Amerikkka? Or do you glance at the floor in silence waiting for the conversation to shift, hoping the racist commentary does not persist for too long, so you can get back to that nice feeling? Como el refrán dice, "the revolution starts at home" mi gente. If we can't address our own anti-blackness with family and friends, how can we possibly fight racism in a larger white supremacist society? It can feel hard, and yes, we risk possibly losing a sense of connection for the moment. But all freedom requires risk and not taking that risk comes at the expense of someone else. So with love I say something like, "Oye papi, que es eso? What's that about?" And start a genuine caring conversation about anti-blackness that we too often avoid. The key for me is to say it with the love I have for both Latinxs and black people and not with righteous indignation. In this conversation, I discuss how anti-blackness has been imposed by white supremacy, how we perpetuate it and highlight the commonalities of black and brown struggles in the U.S.

2. I learn and share about the blackness of my history and culture, while recognizing my racial privilege. We usually associate Afro-Latinxs with Brazil, Cuba, the Dominican Republic and Puerto Rico. I am going to dare to generalize and say that most Latinxs outside of these countries would not claim African ancestry or cultural influence. Did you know that Mexico and Peru combined enslaved more Africans than the U.S.? Between 1502 and 1866, of the 11.2 million documented Africans brought to the Americas, only 450,000 arrived in the United States. The rest were brought to Latin American countries. In fact, almost every country in Latin America enslaved Africans, and many of them had sizeable African populations who influenced our cultures. I did not know about the breadth of our African ancestry until I was an adult. Not only do I now know this, but I also talk about it with other Latinxs.

Now if you are not Afro-Latinx you certainly should not go around claiming that you are black. All Latinxs are not black and do not face the same anti-black racism. As a U.S. born Puerto Rican of mostly Spanish (likely Arab or Berber) decent, I am one of the most privileged types of Latinxs in the U.S. I take pride in the fact that my culture has strong African roots, while not confusing racial and cultural identity. I do not face any anti-black racism and have race privilege because of this. It is my job to push back against this privilege by taking up less space and giving up power when working with Afro-Latinxs and black

Americans.

3. **I am visible about my solidarity with black people.** I try to be visible about my unity and love with black family, friends, and community so my Latinx comunidad can see this unity. Visibility of authentic relationships is powerful (the key word here is AUTHENTIC). Have you ever seen the images of the Black Panthers and Young Lords working together? Or read their parallel 10 and 13-point programs? That shit had an impact on our black and brown communities then and it can now.

In order to be visible about solidarity, I actually have to engage in real solidarity. And I don't mean force my desire to have solidarity onto black people without asking if and how it's wanted. Solidarity is not only my decision. It has to be met by another through our own demonstration of love and commitment. One way we can demonstrate love and commitment is by checking each other when anti-blackness arises con nuestra gente.

4. **I am clear that experiencing racism is not the same as experiencing anti-blackness.** Erasing this difference does not help us deal with our anti-blackness. White supremacy and racism in the U.S. affects all POC. Yet it does not affect us the same, nor does state sanctioned violence affect us as harshly as it affects black Americans. I do not mean to create a hierarchy of suffering, but we cannot deny that black people are murdered

by police, unjustly incarcerated, tried as adults when they are youth, and given longer sentences for minor crimes, at higher rates than any other group of people of color in the U.S. (with Latinxs coming in 2nd).

So when a non-black Latinx I know starts blaming black people for their own struggles because this non-black Latinx has succeeded in spite of racism, I highlight our different experiences of racism and the white supremacist myth that if one "good" person of color can make it up the capitalist social ladder then we all can. I also share how my own privilege as a light skinned non-black Latina has provided me with advantages and almost eliminated my risk of being a target of state-sanctioned violence.

This is not a comprehensive list, but rather four person-to-person ways I address anti-blackness with nuestra gente. What are your approaches? Anti-blackness costs both black and Latinx people OUR LIVES. When our numbers are divided, the chances we will be murdered, jailed or deported by white Amerikkka remain high. If we don't deal with our own anti-blackness, la raza's no raza and palante's patras.

¡Palante!

CarmenLeah Ascencio is a public health social worker, community theatre facilitator, trauma-sensitive yoga instructor, educator and proud Boricua 2nd generation queer femme. She is the director of Get Free and the creator of Freedom Labor Love. She speaks and facilitates BGD Get Free workshops at organizations and schools.

A Guide to Celebrating Indigenous Peoples Day

by Taylor Payer

Has your city recently abolished Columbus Day and adopted Indigenous Peoples Day? Are you looking for some ways to celebrate the holiday? While I am not usually in the business of educating folks on Native things (there are plenty of Native folks out here doing this work, I am just not one of them) something about this day has me feeling generous. Lucky for you, I come from a gift-giving culture (you're welcome). Here are some ideas:

1. Find out the name of the tribe(s) whose land you live on and then make sure all your friends and family know that name. Understand that while you did not personally colonize or commit genocide against an entire people you are the benefactor of those legacies of violence and displacement. Know those legacies.

2. Take your newly acquired knowledge of those Indigenous people whose land you are visiting and acknowledge it publicly.

Announce it at work, school, or at some point in your day. Go home and tell your family. Enthusiastically chant it to the people you pass on the sidewalk. Take it to social media and educate the masses. Whose land do you live on and what happened to make your presence on their land possible?

3. Talk to your kids and students about settler colonialism. If you are not familiar with that term use Google or your local library and find some Native-authored books that will explain it to you. Understand that while some folks came to settle in the United States under forcible displacement, relocation, the need to live in safety, health, and with adequate material realities, and/or other circumstances outside your control you have a relationship to settler colonialism. Reflect on that relationship.

4. Support your local Native businesses and artists by buying their work and visiting their shops, galleries, and restaurants. Go online and buy Native (not "Native- inspired") art, music, and books. Make a donation to your favorite Native non-profit whose invaluable work our communities depend on. My ideas include The Native Youth Sexual Health Network, Winona LaDuke Honor the Earth, and the Native Scholars – American Indian College Fund, but there are many more great organizations out there you can and should support with your cash donations, time, and resources.

5. If you attend a university or other public/private institution whose history with Natives is particularly racist know that history. Educate yourself. Do not ask your token Native friend to explain it to you, but be thankful and self-critical if and when they do. When the inevitable racist comment is made in your class discussion or daily conversations take on the emotional labor of disputing it so that the Native students and others do not have to.

6. Send a letter or text or email to that special Indigenous person in your life and congratulate them for surviving 500+ years of colonialism. Hug a Native friend, permitting you have their consent. Kiss that Native cutie you've been eyeing and if they kiss you back consult this essay to learn how to engage your decolonial love muscles. This way you will have some tools to become a less oppressive date/partner:

7. Burn your "Navajo-inspired" panties, boycott your Urban Outfitters, and work through your attachment to the dream catcher hanging above your bed or the racist mascot on your shirt.

8. Read and think deeply about the unsettling, large, and often ignored number of Indigenous women who are missing, murdered and sexually assaulted. Know the names of trans Native women who are too often the targets of physical, spiritual, and sexual violence. There are Native organizations, artists, and activists doing vital anti-violence and feminist work. Find their

work on social media and help uplift it. If your liberation is inextricably bound with ours then, please, work with us.

9. Go ahead and attend your local Indigenous Peoples Day ceremony or anti-Columbus Day rally. When you do, remember to take up less space and ask yourself how you can better be in solidarity with Native people, struggles, and triumphs. After you are done asking yourselves, ask your communities what you can do to collectively contribute to Indigenous land reclamation projects, language revitalization programs, and more generally uplift the voices of Native peoples. When given the opportunity, listen to Native people and engage with our means of asking for what we need and want. Native communities are the best equipped to articulate what we need from non-Native folks trying to be in solidarity and our right to self-determination is entirely our own. While your support of Indigenous people is graciously accepted your patronizing claps and/or approval is not. Challenge yourselves and your loved ones to learn your relationship to settler colonialism. Be more critical, loving people.

10. Finally, commit to doing this work every day not just when it's a federal holiday. After all, when you live on Turtle Island, every day is Indigenous Peoples Day.

Taylor Payer is Anishinaabe from the Turtle Mountain Indian Reservation in North Dakota. A recovering Ivy League graduate and underemployed legal advocate, she currently resides in Minneapolis, Minnesota. When not working or reading the latest queer theory, you can find her biking around a lake, gawking at art, or roasting vegetables.

Calling IN: A Less Disposable Way of Holding Each Other Accountable

by Ngọc Loan Trần

I started having conversations on this practice of "calling in" after attending Race Forward's Facing Race Conference in Baltimore, MD in 2012. Facing Race was a gathering of thousands of people working on advancing racial justice. The space was full of energy, commitment, and a ride-or-die-and-put-it-all-on-the-line mentality for making sure we've got our bases covered in this fight against racism and dismantling white supremacy.

What happens when thousands of people who all "get it" come together and everyone knows something about "the work"? We lose all compassion for each other. All of it.

I witnessed all types of fucked up behavior and the culture that we have created to respond to said fucked up behavior.

Most of us know the drill. Someone says something that supports the oppression of another community, the red flags pop up and someone swoops in to call them out.

But what happens when that someone is a person we know

— and love? What happens when we ourselves are that some-one?

And what does it mean for our work to rely on how we have been programmed to punish people for their mistakes?

I'll be the first person and the last person to say that anger is valid. Mistakes are mistakes; they deepen the wounds we carry. I know that for me when these mistakes are committed by people who I am in community with, it hurts even more. But these are people I care deeply about and want to see on the other side of the hurt, pain, and trauma. I am willing to offer compassion and patience as a way to build the road we are taking but have never seen before.

I don't propose practicing "calling in" in opposition to calling out. I don't think that our work has room for binary thinking and action. However, I do think that it's possible to have multiple tools, strategies, and methods existing simultaneously. It's about being strategic, weighing the stakes and figuring out what we're trying to build and how we are going do it together.

So, what exactly is "calling in"? I've spent over a year of trying to figure this out for myself, and this practice is still coming to me daily. The first part of calling each other in is allowing mistakes to happen. Mistakes in communities seeking justice and freedom may not hurt any less but they also have possibility for transforming the ways we build with each other for a new, better world. We have got to believe that we can transform.

When confronted with another person's mistake, I often think about what makes my relationship with this person important. Is it that we've done work together before? Is it that I know their politics? Is it that I trust their politics? Are they a family member? Oh shit, my mom? Is it that I've heard them talk about patience or accountability or justice before? Where is our common ground? And is our common ground strong enough to carry us through how we have enacted violence on each other?

I start "call in" conversations by identifying the behavior and defining why I am choosing to engage with them. I prioritize my values and invite them to think about theirs and where we share them. And then we talk about it. We talk about it together, like people who genuinely care about each other. We offer patience and compassion to each other and also keep it real, ending the conversation when we need to and know that it wasn't a loss to give it a try.

Because when I see problematic behavior from someone who is connected to me, who is committed to some of the things I am, I want to believe that it's possible for us to move through and beyond whatever mistake was committed.

I picture "calling in" as a practice of pulling folks back in who have strayed from us. It means extending to ourselves the reality that we will and do fuck up, we stray and there will always be a chance for us to return. Calling in as a practice of loving each other enough to allow each other to make mistakes; a practice of loving ourselves enough to know that what we're trying to do here is a radical unlearning of everything we have been configured to believe is normal.

And yes, we have been configured to believe it's normal to punish each other and ourselves without a way to reconcile hurt. We support this belief by shutting each other out, partly through justified anger and often because some parts of us believe that we can do this without people who fuck up.

But, holy shit! We fuck up. All of us. I've called out and been called out plenty of times. I have gotten on people ruthlessly for supporting and sustaining oppression and refusing to listen to me. People have gotten on me about speaking to oppressions that aren't mine, being superficial about inclusion, and throwing in communities I'm not a part of as buzzwords. But when we shut each other out we make clubs of people who are right and clubs of people who are wrong as if we are not more complex than that, as if we are all-knowing, as if we are perfect. But in reality, we are just really scared. Scared that we will be next to make a mistake. So we resort to pushing people out to distract ourselves from the inevitability that we will cause someone hurt.

And it is seriously draining. It is seriously heartbreaking. How we are treating each other is preventing us from actually creating what we need for ourselves. We are destroying each other. We need to do better for each other.

We have to let go of treating each other like not knowing, making mistakes, and saying the wrong thing make it impossible for us to ever do the right things.

And we have to remind ourselves that we once didn't know.

There are infinitely many more things we have yet to know and may never know.

We have to let go of a politic of disposability. We are what we've got. No one can be left to their fuck ups and the shame that comes with them because ultimately we'll be leaving ourselves behind.

I want us to use love, compassion, and patience as tools for critical dialogue, fearless visioning, and transformation. I want us to use shared values and visions as proactive measures for securing our future freedom. I want us to be present and alive to see each other change in all of the intimate ways that we experience and enact violence.

I want our movements sustainable, angry, gentle, critical, loving—kicking ass and calling each other back in when we stray.

Ngọc Loan Trần is a Viet/mixed-race disabled queer writer grounded in the U.S South. Their work is about bold, fearless visioning that cuts through the nonsense to make real the freedom, justice and love we seek. You can read more of their work and writing at nloantran.com.

3 Things I Regret Not Asking From Allies and My Community As An (Un)Documented and Queer Activist

by Alan Pelaez Lopez

I arrived to the San Diego border at the age of 5, alone, to reunite with my mother, who had been working for a White Mexican family in the United States as a domestic worker and nanny for about 2 dollars an hour, and working 60+ hours a week.

At the age of 5, all I knew is that ma and I were safe here. Ma and I were going to live. I knew that there would be no more family deaths, no more visits to the hospital because of an abusive night at home, but it also meant no more visits to the cemetery to see my younger sister.

Growing up, I knew ma and I were undocumented. I knew that there were people out in the US/Mexican border with rifles shooting migrants, I knew that people didn't want us in the US, I knew all of this, and I learned to survive and to grow up fast.

When I was a teenager, I began to hear about undocumented youth in California, Arizona and New York speaking out in public and sharing their stories as undocumented. As a teenager, I didn't know I had a story, and yearned to be a part of this movement. When I was 16, I joined the undocumented movement and finally felt like I could create change.

Undocumented Afro-Latinx womyn in Boston, and undocumented queer and trans activists, influenced my politics, my art, and my ambitions. While revolutionary people surrounded me, I endured a lot of pain because I didn't know how to hold allies, community members, or myself accountable.

As a queer and (un)documented activist, here are 3 things I regret not doing to hold allies, my community, and myself accountable:

1. I often felt I couldn't say "No" when I was asked to share my story at rallies, public hearings, church talks, community events, or at delegations.

The reason why undocumented youth were able to mobilize so successfully is because undocumented youth took risks: undocumented youth created a national community by sharing their stories of survival, of resistance, and of home. However, as someone with extreme PTSD caused by an interfamily murder, and a history of abuse for not being "man" enough as a toddler, sharing my story often caused me secondary trauma.

To my undocumented community out there, be careful. Your story is yours, and you should not justify every part of your existence. Share what you are comfortable with, and let people know when you need someone else to speak.

To those in solidarity with the undocumented community: the stories you hear are not yours to re-tell. Yes, you should share articles, videos & art by undocumented migrants, but you should not re-tell their stories without their permission. By re-telling their stories you may trigger other migrants; and you may also romanticize and exaggerate stories, thus reducing (and detaching) the lived experiences of those who have so vulnerably shared their truths with you.

2. When people asked me to speak at colleges and universities, galas, or art venues, I always said yes, but never got paid.

Truth be told, undocumented activists are being burnt out, and fast, because a lot of people want to hear our truths, our cuentos, our laughs, our love, but no one wants to pay us for our time.

I remember once traveling about 2 hours on public transit, getting to a college, the facilitator being late, and then being in a panel followed by a Q&A, and all I got for it were a water bottle and chocolate. For real? You're telling me that I just traveled 2 hours, talked for an hour about how undocumented folk are paid less than minimum wage, harassed at work, denied health care, threatened with deportation, and you can't compensate me for my time, but you have a budget for snacks, set-up, cleanup, and tons of fancy posters and invitations?

To my undocumented activists, do not be afraid to demand

compensation for your time. Our truths are not readily available to anyone who wants them. I know that sometimes, we feel that we have to say yes because our stories are barely shared, but you have the right to be treated with respect and consideration. Your stories matter, your time matters, and your money matters.

To those in solidarity with undocumented activists, and to those who work in organizations that serve the undocumented community: if you are going to have an undocumented individual speak somewhere, compensate them. Think about it this way: when you ask someone to speak, they have to write their talk down, they have to revise it, they have to remember many painful memories, then they have to rehearse. Umm, no, this is not free.

3. I regret the most not disclosing to my undocumented community and those in solidarity with us that I was often hungry at our organizing meetings, or scared of my hour and a half commutes at night.

As an (un)documented activist, there was always something more important to do than eating: stopping someone's deportation, fighting for stolen wages from domestic workers, dealing with family issues back in our home countries, etc.

Food and transportation for undocumented and queer activists are major concerns, especially for undocumented queer and trans youth, who are sometimes not privileged to be accepted at home, and thus end up raising themselves in the homes of other undocumented activists, in the streets, or in homeless shelters (if they don't require an ID).

To my undocumented community, it is not shameful to admit that you are hungry, or that you need a ride, or someone to wait for you at the bus stop. I regret not asking for help. Take my advice, if you can, and ask for help when you need it.

To my undocumented community members with modest jobs, and to those who are in solidarity with the undocumented community: please always try to ask undocumented activists if they have eaten, and if you have a car, always offer a ride, if you are able.

Before moving to California, when I was able, I would buy three $15 grocery store gift cards when I went shopping, and whenever I had the chance to give one out to an undocumented activist, I would. Hey, when I worked in the kitchen of a restaurant, and barely made minimum wage, $15 got me a long way at the market.

Just remember that sometimes the best way to be an ally is to allow an undocumented activist to stop for a second, and eat, or to simply ask them if they need a ride. And if you are comfortable with buying gift cards for those in the movement, I would highly suggest it!

Alan Pelaez Lopez is a formerly undocumented Black Mexican artist, contributing writer at Everyday Feminism, *and former* BGD *intern. They currently live in the SF Bay Area where they spend their time making jewelry, reading for grad school, and doing community work with* Familia: Trans Queer Liberation Movement.

Solidarity Struggle Café
"If He Was Black..."

drawn by Ethan Parker

written by Mia McKenzie

Ethan Parker is a self-taught illustrator and comic artist from Austin, TX. He's worked hand-in-hand with Strong Families, Black Lives Matter, and Culture Strike to create visual noise and draw attention to relevant social topics affecting the intersections of Black personhood and queer, trans communities. Ethan is a geeky guy who loves to read comics, play video games and kick flip for social justice.

ETHAN PARKER & MIA MCKENZIE

When Every Summer Is Your Own Personal "Summer Of Sam"

by Shaadi Devereaux

Recently, after one of those weekly conversations where your mother asks if you're dating anyone, I decided I deserved the dairy therapy. On my way back from getting ice cream, I noticed a guy following me from the shop. Another two blocks and suddenly he appeared again, heading me off from around the corner. My alarms were raised. He said he recognized me from 'before' at a community event where I had discussed being a trans woman. I picked up the pace, hoping he would get the hint. My heart racing, I took off my heels and decided to take my chance with the pavement. I passed the police station. I had already gotten into it with the local cops when they profiled me for sex work for being out too late, while waiting for the pedestrian light to change on my way home from work. I made it back, chained my door and decided a new route home was needed. No more frivolous trips. Work, grocery store, home. No more heels. Only trainers.

There have already been six murders of girls like me this year and it's only March. As the weather gets warmer and dreams of summer fill the air, I wonder: what do you do when every summer is your own personal Summer of Sam?

Along with the barbecues and booty shorts, headlines of girls like us being found in dumpsters, and dumped in rivers, pepper the headlines of our local papers.

It seems like as a country we would be horrified. Instead, we remain unfazed. We go to summer concerts as a grizzly murder novel occurs all around us.

There is a peace, stillness and acceptance that occurs around it that is almost as frightening as the violence. It's the makings of horror novels set in dystopian futures. Except there is no clever hero to figure it out and save the day. There are only more bodies in more pieces, forgotten names, and fetishizing headlines. Our city landfills become a cemetery, holding the stories of girls taken out like the weekly trash.

Our names are not only forgotten in the ways of other missing and murdered women, filling the backlogs of unprocessed police reports and tucked away in boxes in a forensics department, but we're erased as women as well. Journalists name us as men in the interest of "journalistic integrity." They scour birth records to include birth names to center the sensation of our bodies over their disappearances. It's a special kind of violence and cowardice to take away our names and call us men when we can no longer speak because our voices lay at the bottom of rivers.

America becomes a fine-tuned machine, a factory with each line of the conveyor belt playing its role in the disappearance of girls like me. Girls who are Black, who are women, and who are trans. We are America's Black Dahlia. Except no one wonders were we went.

From girlhood, trans women are exposed to these layers of violence. What does this look like when it's played out in real time? A fifteen-year-old Black trans girl was recently stabbed at a train station in DC by an adult male. Her friends fended off the attacker with mace and led the authorities to him. News outlets reported the following narrative: a woman (not a girl) stabbed in a train station. There was little mention or praise of the fifteen-year-old heroes who both fended off a full grown attacker with a criminal history and brought him to justice. No highly visible rallies, no big media reports, no town hall meetings. Only an erasure of girlhood and, in several cases, fumbling journalists struggling to describe "a boy who is a trans girl dressed as a woman in girl's clothing." Where is the collective outrage at the serial murder of girls barely old enough to buy a metro pass? As violence expands into our adulthood, how can we keep ourselves safe?

But who exactly is this Jack the Ripper? We are immediately confronted with the two images most commonly reported: the faceless perpetrator of transphobia, committing violent acts with little or no prior relation to the victim, as in the cases of Cece McDonald and Islan Nettles; and men "rightfully defending their sexuality."

In a society that views all non-male bodies through the lens of the male gaze, trans women are often viewed as "traps." The narrative goes that we trick unsuspecting men into lusting after us. Our bodies are perversions waiting to corrupt their masculinity and "normal" sexualities. Any violence is then justified as "panic" and men protecting themselves from the lethal bite of the trans girl werewolf.

But we must also examine the danger in honing in on and sensationalizing the image of either a faceless murderer dripping in 'unexplainable' transphobic bloodlust or the guy who brings home a date that ends in a surprise "trans panic." It erases the all too common experience of intimate partner violence and erases us as victims of this violence as well. If the danger remains an unspoken and mysterious thing in the night, just part and parcel of being a trans woman, then we don't direct our actions, services, and narratives to actively provide resources for these women. Violence against trans women becomes normalized. Our lives are seen as inherently full of violence, with little that can ultimately be done.

Domestic violence and IPV are largely erased in the context of trans women of color because society operates on the logic that intimacy with black trans women never occurs and, if it does, it's a horrifying and abnormal experience. The fact that trans women are in intimate relationships is actively erased and any occurrence of intimate partner violence is immediately replaced with the narrative of "He didn't know. He was tricked. Of course he reacted that way."

Even if a potential partner didn't know, killing a trans woman is an incredibly outsized and violent response. It's a defense that only holds if you believe trans women's bodies can violate non-trans bodies just through association. The crime is the TWoC's body itself, not the act of violence against her. Our bodies are seen as the initial assault.

This idea of criminal bodies, Black and Trans, extends even further into the criminal justice system. When sex work, one of the few lines of work TWoC have access to when they are discriminated against in other forms of employment, is made illegal, and Black and Indigenous genders are seen as inherently sexual and criminal, we are inherently made into a profile. Media narratives pair unconfirmed and unsubstantiated stories of sex work with stories of disappearances, and then imply sex work means 'you brought it on yourself.' Again, we are denied victimhood.

This constant preoccupation with justifying the murders of trans women acts to erase society's responsibility for the culture of violence it creates. It erases the fact that your sons hit on trans women and often respond violently, verbally or physically, when rejected or confronted with the reality of our bodies; that you create a culture of ridicule, entitlement, confusion and fear around interacting with and dating trans bodies; that your daughters take part in the process of outing trans women to possible perpetrators, to leverage and enforce hierarchies of womanhood, to "protect" them from the "trick", and in fact often find it a source of entertainment. It erases the Jerry Springers and the Maurys who sensationalize us. It erases the fact that TWoC are often murdered in the interest of protecting men's honor and guarding their sexuality. It erases the fact that we are turned away from shelters and vital resources with the mantra that we aren't "real women." Every narrative centered around TWoC's lives historically has said that we must have deserved it. If Hester Prynne bore the scarlett letter, then Black Trans women bear the Scarlett Alphabet.

As we seek to take back control over reoccurring narratives of violence in our lives, we look to Mariame Kaba's framework and are reminded that only some of us are seen as having a self to defend. How we recreate the "self" and whose is worth love and defense will mark our anti-violence feminist revolution. If we can successfully fill in the cracks and keep the most vulnerable women safe, we will have a ready system and language in place to tackle the violence we face as a collective whole.

Our success in the rest of the century will be marked by whose victimhood and agency we honor in the crafting of our new world.

Shaadi Devereaux is a Black and AfroIndigenous writer using media to build narratives for Trans Women of Color. She is also an independent contractor and consultant on Women's Global Initiatives and Human Rights.

Asian Americans Benefit From Black Struggle and We Need To Start Shouldering The Burden

by Ally Ang

On November 20th, 2014, a 28-year-old unarmed Black man named Akai Gurley was shot and killed by NYPD officer Peter Liang. The officer, who was later indicted on charges of assault and manslaughter, was said to have discharged his gun accidentally because he panicked upon hearing a noise in the darkened stairwell.

This was one of countless instances of police brutality against black Americans, but this incident in particular caused a stir within the Asian American community because Officer Liang was Chinese. Many Chinese Americans in the community rallied in support of Liang, arguing that he would not have been indicted if he had been white.

To me, this was an example of a long history of Asian Americans derailing necessary conversations around anti-blackness. Of course, Asian Americans are also victims of racial violence. Just look at the murder of Vincent Chin and the countless attacks on South Asian Americans in the post-9/11 racist frenzy. And there is also a large diaspora of black Asians in the United States and across the globe who face anti-blackness from both within and outside of the Asian community at large. But non-black Asians are not subjected to the systematic and government-sanctioned murder of our people in the way that black people are. A few months ago in my tiny hometown of East Lyme, Connecticut, my father (an immigrant from Indonesia) was verbally assaulted and told to "go back to his country" by an off-duty police officer. Rightfully outraged, my father recounted the incident to me, saying, "The police are all racist against minorities!"

"That's true," I responded, "but if you were black, there's a good chance you would be dead right now."

Not all oppression is created equal. The harsh truth is that even though we experience racism in deeply painful and traumatic ways, we are settlers on stolen land just like white people. This nation would not exist without the enslavement and subjugation of black people, and we as Asian Americans have often been complicit in the continuation of their oppression.

In two of the earliest Supreme Court cases regarding the citizenship of people of color, the plaintiffs argued that as Japanese and Indian Americans respectively, they were both closer to whiteness than Black or Indigenous people, and they were therefore more suited to be American citizens than other racial minorities. For many years, Asian Americans have attempted to claim whiteness and "model minority" status, often throwing black people under the bus along the way.

Even though we face problems such as underrepresentation, racial stereotypes, and discrimination, the racism that we face is inextricably linked to anti-blackness. You know the stereotype of Asian Americans being emotionless math geniuses who get perfect SAT scores and become valedictorians at Ivy League universities? It formed as a counterpart to the stereotypes of black and brown people as lazy and underachieving. Anti-blackness is at the very core of the model minority myth, and there are countless examples of Asian Americans perpetuating anti-blackness: from Vijay Chokalingam to the murder of Latasha Harlins to when an Asian American fraternity at UC Irvine posted a video featuring its members in blackface.

However, there is also a very strong legacy of Black and Asian solidarity. Two of the most famous Asian American activists, Yuri Kochiyama and Grace Lee Boggs, are known for their involvement in the Black Power Movement. In one of the most moving moments in history, Kochiyama cradled Malcolm X's head as he lay dying after being shot. But since then, there have been very few Asian American activists who have been so prominently invested in solidarity with black people. It's time to change that.

This is my call to action, my plea for us as a community to follow in the footsteps of our activist foremothers and to start practicing true solidarity. As a light-skinned, mixed race Asian American woman, I am very privileged in a lot of ways. One example of my privilege is that when I read about the deaths of

Sandra Bland, Freddie Gray, Walter Scott, or any of the other horrifying instances of police brutality against black people, I am outraged instead of terrified. I am able to voice my anger, to show up to protests, to loudly condemn the racist criminal justice system because I will not be its next victim. That's why when I see non-black Asian Americans preaching solidarity for people of color, I am immediately skeptical. More often than not, the term "people of color" is used to silence black voices and to mask the specific issues that they face. We have gained so much from the struggles of black people; now, it is our turn to help shoulder that burden.

Ally Ang is a queer poet of color whose roots spread across oceans.

Tired of Land Acknowledgments

by Raven Davis

I am constantly questioning my capacity to show support and solidarity for other people of colour when I know very well that, even in the most radical racialized and queer progressive circles, we as Indigenous people are still being erased in every way; our bodies, involvement, history and experiences.

Land acknowledgments have become a necessary but often insincere beginning to any meeting or event. They have become tokenizing, robotic lip-service to check-mark "inclusiveness" on agendas. Despairingly, we are still struggling for participation beyond the confines of opening remarks and drumming invitations.

At times I struggle to show solidarity to others because I'm tired of being tokenized and trivialized by my own queer Indigenous, Black and people of color (QIBPOC) community. I hear people using phrases such as: "Decolonizing QIBPOC Spaces", "Indigenous Rights Matter", "Honouring Indigenous Women, Two-Spirit, Elders, and Children", "Standing in Solidarity with

Indigenous People". However, I rarely see the same groups extending the offer to Indigenous people to organize, lead or participate in their event, protest or organization. What I do hear are the same insults and dismissals over and over again. "There are no Indigenous people here, so the problems don't exist here" or "we don't hire Indigenous people because they don't apply" or "that happened long ago" or "the government gives you guys everything" or "don't you know, there are others who suffer just as much?"

I've noticed that Facebook and Twitter have increased activist bandwagon-jumping, and so less effort is placed on meaningful solidarity. So many people "like" or repost articles just because they have catchwords in the title such as "Indigenous" or "Treaty Rights," but actually have no idea what they're posting or what it means, and could not speak to it in a conversation outside of social networking

I realize that the school system doesn't educate people about Indigenous issues in their own backyards. I often wonder: how can I expect or encourage people to be more supportive if they don't take the time or care to learn about current issues and the history of Indigenous people?

We are plagued by anti-Indigenous racism. Our fights continue for safety on and off reserves, in our cities, by our law enforcement and child services departments; for our inherent rights to this land, how we fish, gather, live or move; and for our access to safe spaces, economic freedom, proper healthcare, food, housing, employment, education and culturally restorative resources such as language.

Throughout my life, I found it easier to support other POC and specifically Black people's struggles. People got it, at least in my social and academic circles. I learned enough from school, friends and family to understand that Black struggles are real and alive today. Much like Indigenous peoples' struggles, the fight for Black survival and self determination has endured for centuries.

People get it when we talk about land dispossession in countries far from Canada, such as Palestine and Israel. Our streets are full of protest supported by allies for these fights, yet Indigenous people still struggle to get a mere 200 people to a protest in a city that has been settled by millions of people. Where is the support for our fight?

When people think about Indigenous issues, they often assume these issues no longer need to be addressed. I'm confident most of my non-Indigenous friends haven't even been to a reserve for anything other than gas or cigarettes. I'm also pretty sure I am their only Indigenous friend. How many of my hundreds of social network "friends" who post article after article about other activist issues have supported an Indigenous protest? Or have challenged family members on their understanding of current Indigenous issues? How many have read the government sanctions on Indigenous lives in this country? How many have fought to raise awareness about Indigenous reserves? These reserves were based on the same framework as concentration camps and still operate in third world conditions.

In school, we were taught about the Underground Railroad, the Holocaust, Slavery, World Wars I and II, the "discovery of North America," Vikings, the Irish famine, the medieval times, the Roman Empire. It's easy to rhyme off these historical events, but we are unaware of genocide of Indigenous people in Canada and the United States. We are brainwashed to believe that Indigenous people died because of weak immune systems and cold weather. We are taught that "Indians" are dirty, stupid, primitive and a burden to our governments. We don't learn about the slavery of Indigenous lives. We don't learn about enfranchisement, which is the forced surrender of Indian Status. We don't learn about how the government manipulated young, Indigenous, unwed women to give up their babies during the 60's. In school, my children don't learn about the third world living conditions on reserves now, or how many people don't have running water or proper housing. Instead we are taught that all Indigenous people live in teepees and igloos, hunt buffalo and dance by fires.

How can we expect people to stand in solidarity with us when they don't know a thing about Indigenous people? Some of my friends are overwhelmed by the subject of Indigenous struggle and see Indigenous problems as "federal government issues." They don't understand our issues and, for the most part, turn their backs when I try to make space to talk about them.

Recently, a QIBPOC friend of mine posted on social media

about her lack of connection to Toronto and said she never felt "home" to any of the places she's resided in Canada. Within minutes, people began posting about their "hate" for certain cities—how they've never felt connected, how ugly these cities are compared to their own "homes" and how they will never feel at home in these places—and the post became very well-circulated. Although all these feelings are valid, in all of the posts they were talking about one thing: Indigenous land. They were talking about my territory, my home. They were talking about land Indigenous people don't have a legal right to, that we continue to fight for.

I spent the whole day reading post after post and, finally, I couldn't take it anymore. I replied in the thread validating their feelings but also suggesting that when people speak about "land" and specifically in this settler state, that they become more aware of their privilege as people living on this land, and to be mindful: their hateful complaints about the land might fall on Indigenous ears.

Within two minutes of me posting my reply, my friend deleted the whole post. She wrote me personally thanking me for my comment and agreed that it was wrong to post. I was grateful that she wrote and apologized to me. However, I was terribly sad when my voice and opinion stopped at her. No one else got to read what I posted. No one else got to learn something so valuable because she deleted it. Why? This is exactly what's done to our voices every day: they are erased.

Something shifts in me when I think about solidarity with other POC. I want to support my extended IBPOC family and all their issues because I believe that they are fighting similar fights as us. The betrayal seems huge when we don't get support from our own QIBPOC community. When we look for it and people don't show up.

I want to encourage solidarity that flows deeper than land acknowledgments. I want us to start building our meetings, events and agendas with the voices of Indigenous people on the panels and in the keynotes, rather than just the opening prayers. I want us to rethink how often we use the word "decolonize" and what that actually means to us individually. I want us to consider what type of activists we would be if Facebook didn't exist. How do you support Indigenous people beyond acknowledging your privilege and reciting a land acknowledgment? What are you doing to decolonize and reconcile with Indigenous people?

I want us to truly decolonize our most radical QIBPOC spaces right in our own backyards. I want spaces in QIBPOC circles where we talk about the oppression and violence against Indigenous lives. I want Indigenous issues to be a priority. I want to talk about this land and the Indigenous people belonging to it. I want people to be proud to say they are indigenous to other places without watering down the Indigenous struggles of this land. I want dedicated help with reclaiming sovereignty to this land. I want meaningful Indigenous involvement, leadership, solidarity and inclusion. I want more than just a land acknowledgment.

Raven Davis is an Indigenous, mixed race, 2-Spirit multidisciplinary artist and activist from the Anishnawbek (Ojibwa) Nation. A parent of 3 sons, Raven's work includes performance, painting, design, poetry and short film. Raven blends narratives of colonization, race and gender justice, 2-Spirit identity and the Anishinaabemowin language and culture into traditional and contemporary art forms.

Immigrants in Solidarity with Indigenous People

Dedicated, with love, to Raven

by Elisha Lim

Learning about Native Canadian history has put me on the defensive. I'm in love with you, so I wanted to learn about your people. But I now feel as though I don't know who my own people are anymore. Are we greedy immigrants grasping at our piece of the colonial pie? It makes me upset, angry and resentful.

You made a video called "It's Not Your Fault," about missing and murdered Aboriginal women and Two-Spirit people. It went viral immediately. It focused on public reactions to the announcement that, after one hundred years of ignoring the epidemic of violence against Aboriginal women, there was going to be an inquest on the subject. The video featured you praying in a thoughtful, understated way. I told that to everyone except you. I don't think you heard me say a single nice thing about it.

I was similarly reluctant to look up what you said about slavery.

"You know, there were more Native slaves than Black slaves in Canada."

"Jesus, that's bleak."

But the numbers were shocking. In 1759, out of the approximately 3,500 slaves in Canadian New France, 2,472 were Indigenous. More than two-thirds, because Indigenous people were sold for half the cost of other enslaved people.

I've been better able to express my sympathy in my university elective course, Contemporary Indigenous Canadian Art. I was instantly grieved when the first Indigenous professor I've ever had taught us that the reason we have no sense of Indigenous history is that Indigenous people weren't allowed to go to university until recently. Under Section 112 of the Indian Act, anyone who wanted to pursue higher education had to renounce their treaty and statutory rights as Native people and give up their right to return home to their reserve. This section of the act was removed in 1961, but for another decade, even Native students who were offered university admission would need the permission of a generally uncooperative Indian Agent, who was a European bureaucrat tasked with managing Indian affairs in their respective district. Professor Devine sighed, "these Indian Agents were typically European farmers and trappers who lived and worked in competition with the same Native people they were managing, eh?"

Professor Devine would later weep as she told the story of Alex Janvier, a Dene Suline painter who inspired Canada's contemporary Indigenous art movements. In the 1950s, Janvier was the first Indigenous artist to gain acceptance into my university.

His Indian Agent forbade him from enrolling and sent him to a technical school instead.

Even worse, she went on to explain, in 1885 the Indian Act actively criminalized the artistic traditions of Native people. The Royal Canadian Mounted Police would arrest any Native person for carving poles, crafting masks, or creating any ceremonial object, from totem poles to regalia. This led to the "kitschification" of Indigenous art, as European merchants started the swift and lucrative wholesale of Native artwork. I naively asked professor Devine what made this trade so lucrative. She paused, surprised that the answer wasn't obvious to me. "Because after this law, it was all going extinct," she answered. It reminded me of your German boss and his insatiable appetite for the traditional paintings you produced. I choked.

I was jealous, though, when Professor Devine invited you to screen your film in our class, and she called you an artistic genius. A couple of students had seen it before and declared that your work makes them cry. But I was so proud when you answered everyone's questions marvelously. You laughed your handsome, golden laugh. You put your foot down when someone demanded the right to use the word "Indian." And every time you looked over at me, your gaze was full of love.

That day Professor Devine assigned us the essay "Decolonization is Not a Metaphor" by Eve Tuck and KW Yang, authors who are Native and Chinese, respectively, like you and me. It totally messed me up. I was shocked and grieved to read the section entitled "Moves to Innocence," where the authors tackle the case study of Asian immigrants.

> Minority literature preoccupied with "glass ceilings" and "forever foreign" status and "myth of the model minority" offers a strong critique of the myth of the democratic nationstate. However, its logical endpoint, the attainment of equal legal and cultural entitlements, is actually an investment in settler colonialism. Indeed, even the ability to be a minority citizen in the settler nation means an option to become a brown settler.

I can't help but feel a dark sense of amusement when white people grieve about racism, because the recognition of their entitlement is long overdue. But I am not ready to come to terms with my own unearned privileges. It's already so easy to hate Chinese people on this continent. We are depicted as insensible, smelly, ignorant, passive, back-stabbing, cat-eating, cheap plastic knock-off breeding child accountants. Can't I have a break?

But at this point, Tuck and Yang were just getting started with their argument. Any discussion of colonialism, they argued, must address settler colonialism. Land acknowledgments must address Indigenous sovereignty and rights. Decolonization isn't just a way to rewrite the syllabus while keeping one's job. The idea of decolonization isn't a formula for holistic self-awareness and interconnectivity. The fact is, immigrants are occupiers, holding down land that is the bounty of genocide.

The colonial government allotted your people only two percent of the land we call Canada. Native people face eighty-nine percent unemployment rates. They occupy thirty percent of the jail population, fifty percent of the foster system and breathtaking rates of mental illness, addiction and suicide. Metaphorically "decolonizing" my art gallery won't relieve your crisis. You need your lives back. When Tuck and Yang say, "Decolonization is not a Metaphor," they are saying that decolonization means literal repatriation, nothing less. "All of the land, and not just symbolically."

I phoned you and I cried like a baby.

"My class readings are asking me to leave the country, but I don't know where I belong."

"I don't want you to leave," you said.

Of course, I understand the injustice: at the end of this Indigenous course, I, unlike you, will be given a master's degree. In my desperation for some measure of equity, I've started reading you my homework. Last week I read you an essay by Leanne Betasamosake Simpson.

Kwezens is out walking in the bush one day

It is Ziigwan

the lake is opening up

the goon was finally melting she's feeling that first warmth of spring on her cheeks "Nigitchi nendam, she is thinking, "I'm happy."

You laughed at my mispronounced Anishinaabemowin, and said, "I love that you're reading this to me." But eventually I got to the part about Native mothers, and I didn't even think to warn you to brace yourself.

What if the trauma and pain of on-going colonial gendered violence had made it impossible for her mama to believe her or for her mama to reach out and so gently rub her lower back at that critical point?

You started to cry, in that sharp gasping way that made the phone go silent.

It was hard for me to write this essay. I had to ask for an extension. When I finally finished it, I sent it to you and you read it immediately, even though you were driving.

"I like it," you said lovingly.

"Why?"

"Because it feels like an apology."

Elisha Lim is the author of 100 Crushes, *a graphic novel about queer people of colour from around the world. Lim is an award winning claymation filmmaker and illustrator, and is currently writing an MFA that documents a genealogy of Toronto artists of colour.*

Want To Be An Ally To Sex Workers?
Here's What You Need To Understand
by T.S. Piper Darling

Each year on December 17th, International Day to End Violence Against Sex Workers is observed around the world. Even though it is an international event, I want to talk about violence against sex workers in the United States because it has the highest rate of sex worker murders worldwide.

The criminalization of sex work in the United States is largely the reason why it can be so dangerous. Many people hold the idea that harsher policing will 'save' more sex workers, but that approach actually serves to continue violence and destroy many of our tactics for safety. The more that sex work is pushed underground and harshly policed, the more unsafe the work becomes. Instead of relying on the (in)justice system, many of us depend on ourselves, our sex worker communities, and our solidarity networks for support and safety.

Several years ago, I received a violent message from a potential client. He lashed out at me for disclosing that I have sex with men of color. This obviously raised red flags so I immediately stopped responding. While it's common for me to have white clients who are overtly racist, nobody had ever been verbally violent with me before.

Almost a year later, I heard that he'd harmed other trans women sex workers by robbing, attacking, and stalking them. I heard he's even killed a girl. If you are someone who trusts the police, knowing that this happened without anybody stopping him may seem like a fluke. But the truth is, most police really don't take violence against trans women seriously, especially those who are sex workers.

The first thing I learned, from the very first time a client put his hands on me, is that you take your lumps, patch yourself up, move on and add him to a blacklist to let other sex workers know.

But it's not uncommon for sex workers who survive violence to go to the police. Often, this makes the situation worse. Because sex workers are not protected by the law, police get away with being violent against sex workers. Police will make threats for sexual favors.

Women, especially trans women of color, experience cruel treatment from the police, such as being chained to fences, groped, or tossed into jail cells with men who attack or rape them with the implicit blessing of cops. It is not just women who are affected. Men who do sex work are subject to violence too, especially due to homophobia if they're gay.

As sex workers, we've developed our own methods to keep ourselves safe as best we can. From my peers, I've learned to be careful of a client who worships me and not to mistake it as safety. While clients may be sincere in their adoration, it can quickly go sour. The 'worship-murder' scenario most commonly occurs against trans women.

Knowing how it can go wrong is important, just as it is also important to know how we can improve our own safety. The best support and resources are provided by groups organized by sex workers. We've even created blacklist and 'bad date websites' to keep each other, and ourselves, safe from harmful clients. After we've screened our clients, we let friends know where we're going. Some of us hire drivers who take us to our appointments and make sure things go well. While hiring a random driver can be dangerous, having someone that I trust drive me helps me feel safer.

Despite all the work we do towards sex worker safety, there is also a lot of organizing being done that makes things worse for sex workers. Prohibitionists, or people who seek to, in their view, "rescue" sex workers actually make sex work more dangerous. They claim that they have the best interest of sex workers in mind, while simultaneously destroying our safety nets. These "rescue" attempts fail, because criminalization only feeds crime against us.

That said, non-sex workers can and do play important roles in our safety. Sex workers have formed alliances with other groups that offer solidarity, such as queer organizations and drug harm reduction groups. There are many 'allies' who fight hard for us to oppose criminalization. One sex worker organization, Sex Worker Outreach Project, created a resource list for allies.

The biggest step towards showing solidarity with sex workers is to treat us all with dignity. There are many ways to show solidarity with us, like donating to groups like SWOP or Project SAFE, but our allies need to listen to what we have to say first.

It's important that on December 17th, and every day, we respect sex workers. The violence is a byproduct of criminalization and harmful stigmas that we can fight together. This December 17th I want to recognize those we've lost and love those we have here.

TS Piper Darling is a transgender sex worker and sugar baby. Her favorite stores are Sephora, Amoeba Music, and Karmaloop. Her favorite party favors are lipstick and good food. Music and clothes are her oxygen.

Broke on Broke Crime

by Kitzia Esteva-Martinez

I am riding my bike home from visiting a friend and lightly grocery shopping in my neighborhood of San Antonio Park, Oakland. My bike chain falls off so I stop to fix it, as usual, and slowly ride up the hill. There are only five blocks left to go. Three young men, wearing hoodies, walk toward me. It is dark, after 6 P.M., but I can still see them in the distance. It doesn't occur to me to be afraid. I am grateful for their presence, as the neighborhood often feels lonely after sun down. They come at me fast, stop me in the middle of the street, put a gun in my face, and make me give them my things. Moving the gun to my stomach, they search for more things to take. Then, they run away. I don't resist, so it happens quickly, 1, maybe 1.5, minutes. It feels like an eternity.

I can still see it, like a film, rolling millisecond by millisecond. They are so young, so beautiful. The one in front of me, pointing the gun at my face, looks like a deer, not in headlights, but free and majestic. When he first pulls out the gun, I feel rage and reach for my bike lock, ready to blow back. But, then, I get that deja vu feeling, like we've met before, like he could be one of the youth I recruited to join the Bus Riders Union on the buses of L.A., who would get in trouble for selling weed at school, who wanted to join the marines because there were no better opportunities for him. I let go of the bike lock and put it safely back in my basket. With everything happening so fast, they probably didn't even notice my grabbing it. I am more disarmed by their youth than the gun. I am terrified that as they expose themselves by mugging me in the middle of the cop-ridden streets of my neighborhood, they too could be targeted, but by state violence.

When I tell people what had happened, I hear myself choosing words carefully, selectively. I focus, just as much, on my compassion and heartbreak as my resilient rage because people tend to side with the victim and talk about punishment without really thinking of the root causes of the crime, without thinking of the humanity and the conditions of the so-called criminal. When I get home, my roommate and ex-partner, a white, cisdude organizer who identifies as anti-racist, advises me not to call the police, not to engage the prison industrial complex. He tries to make space for me but I feel layers and layers of alienation overwhelming me. I don't know what to do. I let rage take over and text my stolen phone; they text back mockingly. Given that the mugging happened so close to my home, I fear they might know where I live, I fear for my safety. I cave in to the hegemonic assumption that the police will keep me safe and call to report my stolen property. Eventually, after crying and taking a shower, I call it a day and fall asleep.

The police come knocking at 3 A.M., reawakening me to the nightmare and forcing me to relive the trauma as I tell it to them. I am asked to describe the youth. What race where they? Black. How old where they, approximately? 14 to 16. How dark was their skin? Were they wearing baggy clothes? Did they have an afro? As I answer the questions, I feel sick to my stomach for having to tell the police the details of the race and color of already criminalized youth. I feel alienation from these black and brown OPD officers, from those youth, from myself. I don't tell the police, as I don't tell most of my friends, that they called me "Mexican bitch" and taunted me because, at some level, omitting those words makes me feel like I can let them go without internalize them. However, my silence coupled with their deafening words and the threat of violence coupled with youth and poverty are weighty contradictions too heavy for my arms or back to carry.

When my aunt found out I had been mugged, she called me and told me to think about moving back to San Francisco. Despite participating in a Black and Brown unity organization for many years, she is convinced Black folks will continue to "target us." "They like to target the Day Laborers as they come home with their cash in their pockets from work," she tells me. I have heard, a lot of times actually, by other members of my community, of desperate Black folks targeting immigrants, particularly

Latinos, because we are more likely to carry cash than credit. But it goes both ways. I've been robbed on BART by a Latino guy, I've witnessed other Latinos mugging people of color. The fear and animosities between black and brown folks are dangerous, and they help justify the violence of the state and other hateful white groups towards us. At the end of the day, it helps white supremacy. When we see each other as enemies, when we start to accept that our people should be put in cages instead of pushing for real solutions to the poverty and economic, social and state violence we experience we help white supremacy. When I told my neighbor, Michael, a black man in his 50's, what had happened, he told me that he bought a gun because his house was robbed a few years ago. He said, "Tell me if you see them, I'll shoot them on the spot." I reply that I don't want anyone dead. This issue of broke on broke crime is complicated and yet simple. When and where did we learn to see each other as vulnerable and targetable? What have we internalized that we experience each other as hurtable and disposable?

I know the roots of the issue, and I keep them in mind for perspective during the process of decompressing and trying to heal from the trauma. Understanding the systemic reasons for the poverty I was confronted with in my own neighborhood is part of my own fighting-back arsenal, but there is a level of healing that has to happen at a more intimate level. The itchy feeling under my skin that tells me I was targeted because I am a small Latina, that my perceived appearance makes me an easy exploit in their eyes, the nasty feeling of my muscles tightening every time I ride my bike and see three or more black men or youth walking down the block. These feelings bury me deeper in layers of isolation at how easily my body clenches as it takes on the narrative of "Black danger." But this danger is momentarily true in my body as I recover from trauma. Is this reaction a coping mechanism?

In the world we must build, justice would not mean targeting their black bodies with state violence, but an intimate healing of our communities' beef with each other, a conflict that ultimately comes from white supremacy and patriarchy. Justice would be a world where boys of color don't have to mug me to survive, to be men. This work is more nuanced than calling the police, than calling for harsher sentences, than banning weapons. What is needed to heal the alienation between our communities, the isolation from each other, looks like economic justice that we fight for in solidarity and unity. It also looks like intimate justice. Healing the traces and legacies of sexism, colorism, homophobia, anti-black racism, and xenophobia as they manifest in violently intimate and intimately violent ways. Black lives matter, brown lives matter. We must all see this together. We must all do this work together.

Kitzia Esteva-Martinez is an community-organizer, artist, undocumented and queer immigrant mujer for Mexico.

To Be Fat POC & Free

by Quita Tinsley

As a young, queer Black woman, my friends, family, and community have been crucial for my well-being. Honestly speaking, finding a community of queer and trans people of color saved my life. There is something so beautiful and magical about having POC-only spaces to be able to vent and decompress free from white gaze, white guilt, and white tears. There's also something beautiful and magical about having community that validates your lived experiences and confirms that macro- and micro- aggressions and oppressions can be equally impacting on how you navigate your life. One of the most beautiful aspects of having community that reflects your lived experiences is being able to share your experiences without centering whiteness. Having such a brilliant example of POC community and solidarity in my life has left me longing even more for fat people of color.

I think of the powerful impact a fat POC community could have had on me throughout my life. Would I have felt so isolated in my feelings about fatness and body-shaming? Would it have taken me until I was in my 20s to feel comfortable wearing short dresses and skirts? Would I have had as many unhealthy relationships as I did because I thought no one could ever love me and my fat body?

Are there other fat people of color longing for community like me? How can we build together and show up for each other? Can we share tips on chub rub and chest sweat? Can we share strategies on dismantling fatphobia and white supremacy? Can we can learn to listen to our desires of longing and build community and solidarity with each other, whether in person or online? Can we have the pleasure of sitting within the beauty of the magic that we build with each other?

While solidarity has become a buzzword for some, I believe that solidarity is a practice that we must use in our daily lives to move closer to our collective liberation. Practicing solidarity is one of the strategies that we must use in order to work towards dismantling white supremacy and fatphobia. While solidarity looks different for everyone, there are some strategies that I would love to see fat people of color making a part of our common practices of solidarity.

One of these practices is affirmations. We have to be sure to affirm each other more for showing up in the world. Black femmes have shown me the art of affirming one another. Whether it is "yasss-ing" someone down for their amazing outfit or letting someone know that you're glad to see them, affirmations are important because they verbalize to others that we see them.

Another form of affirmation is checking in with people to see how they are. It's important to let each other know that we see each other when we show up in the world, but that we also have value when we're not visibly seen.

While I'm at a point in my life journey where I feel comfortable leaving my house in crop tops and short skirts, I wasn't always at this point. There were some days that I didn't want to leave the house because I was so ashamed of my body and didn't want to be triggered by the potential stares and giggles I might have encountered. Affirming each other strengthens our confidence to show up in a world that wishes to make us smaller. Affirmations also let us know we're not alone when we don't have the strength to show up.

We must also practice having honest conversations and holding each other accountable. We are doing a disservice to each other if we aren't acknowledging the various racializations of our fat bodies; aren't confronting the sizeism and colorism that happens within fat communities; and aren't recognizing the ways in which we are complicit or actively participating in the policing of other fat people of color's bodies. Creating a community of fat people of color is necessary and can be beautiful, but it also has the potential to be triggering and traumatic if we aren't actively unpacking our internalized racism and fatphobia.

Growing up, my mother, a plus size, dark-skinned Black woman, would use the word "sloppy" as a shaming tool to police me into not gaining more weight. Sloppy was a term that she used to judge people who were typically bigger than a size 18/39. This type of thinking is not unique to my mother. It is this same internalized fatphobia and fat-shaming that praises the bodies of plus size people whose bodies seem "height weight proportionate." These are the same types of bodies that are most visible in the body positive movement. Just because we hold marginalized identities as fat people of color doesn't mean that we are exempt from holding oppressive notions. We have to recognize that everyone's bodies, whether they be thick or really fat, are valuable and worthy of love and respect.

While accountability and honesty are crucial, we must also respect where others are in their journeys. We aren't disposable and shouldn't be treated as such if we aren't ready to stand on the front lines of any movements. For example, as mentioned, my mother is someone who taught me to be ashamed of my fat body and shamed me herself. However, as I've grown older and deeper in my own journey of unpacking my shame, I've chosen to speak honestly with her about her language versus shutting her out. While I don't think it's feasible or safe to ask that we all remain in toxic relationships for the sake of not disposing of people, I do think that we have to push ourselves to interrogate what it means to protect ourselves. We have to consider that it's sometimes easier to dispose of problematic people of color than to confront their reflections of our internalized oppression. It could be easy for me to shut my mother out for the ways that she's hurt me, but I also want to teach her how she has hurt me and how to respect my body and me. By choosing to teach her, I am challenging myself to speak up for my own protection and also let her know that I love her enough to let her know when she's wrong. We have to bring this type of love and compassion to our relationships with other fat people of color.

We should also practice building space for each other. It can be easier to find space for ourselves in an oppressive society that wishes to vanish us than to create space *for ourselves and each other*. It is often seen as acceptable to laugh and point at fat people, which I believe influences our hesitance to be seen in groups with other fat people. For example, I'd build relationships with people who I thought were pretty and cool who were most times not understanding of what it meant to be a fat person, because I didn't want to confront my own fatness or have others confront it for me. But what would it look like if we weren't afraid to build intimate and visible relationships with each other? It's important to have community that will navigate life with you publicly. What magic could we create if, as fat people of color, we challenged each other to be seen with each other?

Last, but not least, I think an important solidarity practice is the decentering of whiteness in our conversations about the intersections of fatness and race. As someone who has found much of my voice in writing, I've often turned to the internet to vent my feelings and experiences as a fat person. But most times, I find myself centering whiteness by having to constantly confront the lack of POC visibility within fat and body positive movements. Think-pieces and call-outs are necessary, but also can be draining. I don't want to keep expending energy to convince white people that it's important that fat people of color bodies are reflected if we actually want cultural shift in the realm of body positivity. And I also don't want this to be the only space that fat people of color have on the internet, or in life, to share our experiences. We deserve to have space free from the centering of whiteness. We deserve to have the space to build relationships and community with each other. We deserve to have communities and spaces where we can unpack the internalized shame that has tried to convince us we shouldn't exist as we are.

These practices of solidarity aren't the "end all, be all" of what solidarity for fat people of color should look like, but they are a few examples. I would love to see these and other practices of solidarity be shared to build stronger community with each other. We deserve to experience each other's love, knowledge, and presence. We owe it to ourselves, each other, and our liberation.

Quita Tinsley is a fat, Black, queer femme that writes, organizes, and builds toward liberatory and sustainable change in her home, the Southeast. She is a member of Echoing Ida and serves on the Board of Directors for Access Reproductive Care—Southeast.

Let Us Direct Our Own Lives:
The Importance of Solidarity With Youth of Color
by Kai Minosh Pyle

In my first twelve years of education, I never had a single teacher of color. I admit this absence did not seem strange to me at first: I took for granted the fact that leaders would be white, because I didn't know there was any other way for the world to be. I didn't question the disparity between the diversity of the adults around me, the faces of family and friends, and the pure whiteness of all those involved with teaching young people, those leading us.

It was only in my junior year of high school, as I started to mobilize with other queer and trans youth and youth of color, that I met adults of color actively engaged with youth. That I met queer adults of color—people whose very existence awed me, who for the first time showed me that adulthood did not have to mean assimilation to an oppressive norm that didn't want to accept people like me. In the era of "It Gets Better," I still struggled with whether or not it was possible to have any future at all as a transgender indigenous person.

It's too easy for adults to become wrapped up in their own world that excludes youth of color. The work of community members can become focused on adults, forgetting that most forces that harm adults also harm youth, and that those youth often have fewer resources available to help them. Adult activists may not even realize that youth are organizing on their own—the youth organizing gay-straight alliances in the high schools where I grew up had formed an enormous support network between all the student groups in the city before any adult took notice of us.

This lack of connection with adults of color is painful for youth of color. We begin to wonder, do they really care about us? Isolation and hopelessness can be overwhelming for us. The adults of color around us in our families and friends may be present, but often they don't understand why we are struggling. We need to see adults of color in every aspect of our lives, we need to see adults of color who are trying to change the world.

We need more than just visibility, though. Real connections must be built between adults and youth of color. As mentors, allies, and just as friends. The first adults of color to really try to create that kind of a relationship with me were activists who dedicated part or all of their time to working with youth. Some of them also did other work that was less youth-focused, but they knew that young people needed care and attention. Not just as unformed blank slates to be taught, but as people who have needs like any other person.

Unfortunately, even adults who believe youth matter often make the mistake of imagining us as outsiders who need to be brought in. Instead, you should think of us as actors in our own right, as you would think of other people you reach out to. Remember that we are not: an "at-risk" pool in need of correction. Remember we are not: tokens that can be inserted into the youth slot at your pleasure.

I was once offered the opportunity to join a committee that intended to kickstart a support group for marginalized youth. I jumped at it, excited that adults were interested in hearing from youth ourselves. Then came the meetings—long debates about what was best for young people, how they should go about making this group, while I was the only young person in the room. Sometimes, they would make me stand up and they would proudly tell newcomers, "This is our youth advisor." Our advisor, who speaks when spoken to. Our advisor, who responds so well to the question, "What will the youth think of this?"

Nearly all people of color know the pain of being made a token, of being made to speak for your entire people. Why, then, do adults of color insist on inflicting that pain on youth of color? Perhaps it seems different to them because we are "too young" to make those big decisions that shape the outcome of whatever we are working on. I have no doubt that the adults who think this have good intentions. They want to hear our voices in some form. But underneath their insistences that they want to hear us is the reality that it is more comfortable for them to set the path and have us around to confirm what they're doing is right.

As scary or risky as it may seem, if adults of color want to support youth of color, they need to let us direct our own lives. We need to set the agenda, we need to determine what is important to us. In contrast to the youth group that eventually resulted from the committee I mentioned earlier, another youth group I have been involved in is a model of genuinely respectful youth-adult interactions. This group, composed of indigenous middle school and high school students, decided what issues in the community were most important to them. They defined their goals for the year, they chose what actions they were going to take. The adults provided guidance and helped the youth through figuring out what they needed to do, but it was from the start a youth-led project.

I hear so many older people of color call us "future leaders." I want these folks to realize that many young people are already leaders. If we are given a chance, we will eagerly seize opportunities for leadership. We are leaders among our families and friends, helping those younger than us. We are leaders among our peers, articulating the issues of those around us. And we are even leaders of our communities, speaking in the voice of the youth who are often ignored. In indigenous communities and many other communities of color, people under the age of twenty-five often make up half the population. Our voices and our visions of the future cannot be ignored by anyone truly wishing to make a difference in our communities.

My suggestion for adults wishing to be in solidarity with youth of color is this: recognize the disparity of access and social capital between adults and youth, and do everything you can to bridge the gap. Youth, especially those who are not of legal age, face limits in both tangible resources and in the extent to which they are taken seriously by adults. This is especially true for youth of color, who are disproportionately entangled in systems such as foster care, public education systems, and welfare. Adults of color must be aware of these limits on youth. Below are a few ideas for how adults can act in solidarity with youth of color.

Truly listen to youth of color and amplify our voices. Don't just ask for our input on your ideas, make us a fundamental part of the process from the very beginning. Listen to what we say we need rather than assuming. Value our contributions equally with the contributions of older people. When our voices are nowhere to be seen, seek us out and give us a platform to be heard.

Give us opportunities to lead. Though I have said we are already leaders, it is true that we are still young and because of that we may have less experience than other, older leaders. Because of the power dynamic between youth and adults, we may not be able to practice leadership skills in all situations. Making space for youth to be leaders gives us that chance to develop our leadership so that we will be even greater leaders in the future.

Help us access resources that we otherwise would not be able to. Adults often have access to, or at least know how to access, resources that youth do not, especially when the youth are under legal age. Things like money, cars, and housing are frequently more easily available to adults than to youth. Although it is also true that adults of color are less likely to have this access than white folks, they still have more resources than youth of color. See what we need. See what you can offer us that we cannot get for ourselves.

Connect us with one another and with adults. I have described my own loneliness as a young two-spirit person. For queer and trans youth of color, isolation is a particular danger. I will be forever grateful to the adults who put me in contact with other young activists of color, and with older, experienced activists. Those relationships have endured and blossomed over the years and they have helped me grow as a person and as an activist. These relationships are the kind that we need to build with one another. Only through genuine collaboration between youth and adults of color will our communities have the strength they need to continue fighting.

Kai Minosh Pyle is a Métis two-spirit living on Menominee, Ho-Chunk, and Oneida land. They have worked as an activist, a student, an artist, a youth group member and leader, and a writer. Kai has previously been published in kimiwan zine, and is currently pursuing a PhD in American Studies.

Solidarity Struggle Café
Why Are You Being So Divisive?

drawn by Joamette Gil

written by Mia McKenzie

Joamette Gil is a queer Afro-Cuban illustrator, cartoonist, and writer from the Miami diaspora. Her interdisciplinary degree in social justice and psychology gave her a language to identify the socioeconomic inequities her mom always called "la vida." Now she works everyday to create her own language – a combination of images, words, and digital technologies – to tell the stories she was always waiting for.

JOAMETTE GIL & MIA MCKENZIE

JOAMETTE GIL & MIA MCKENZIE

Any Of Us Could Be Muslim

by Yasmin Begum

London has its first-ever Asian mayor. The son of a bus driver, Sadiq Khan is Muslim and recently won the mayoral election against Zac Goldsmith from the Conservative party. Goldsmith sent out leaflets to many South Asian households insinuating that Khan, from the Labour Party, would be unable to tackle extremism. These leaflets were not sent to Muslim South Asian households or any households with Muslim names. Goldsmith did this as an anti-Muslim smear to pit different people of colour against each other, politically speaking. The claims he made played well into tensions existing between Muslims and non-Muslims of South Asian descent. What is most remarkable, however, is that Goldsmith thought that he could get away with publishing this literature without criticism.

London has the largest population of racialised people in Western Europe, so the election has raised questions about how non-Muslim people of colour practice solidarity with Muslims.

There are roughly 2.7 million Muslims in the United Kingdom and the largest ethnic group among them are South Asians. This is for a whole range of reasons, such as the colonial legacy of the UK in countries such as Pakistan, Bangladesh and India. As a result, Islam in the UK—where I grew up—is linked in the white imagination to a particular (formerly colonised) racial group.

The association of Islam with South Asians in the United Kingdom erases the lived experience of black Muslims and black Islamic heritage. Ten percent of the British Muslim population is Black—a figure that is more than doubled in the United States. Like South Asian Muslims, Black Muslims also face Islamophobia and white supremacy; and they also face anti-blackness from non-Black Muslims.

We are told as a society that Muslims look like people of South Asian and Middle Eastern descent. But as people of colour, any of us could be part of a faith group that has 1.2 billion global adherents worldwide.

Islam, as a religion, is certainly racialised. In fact, Islam is so racialised that people who aren't Muslim become moving targets for Islamophobic abuse. This includes Sikhs—Hindus who frequently wear shalwaar kameez or religious dress (such as turbans) that people may mark out as "Muslim" clothing.

The fear of Muslim bodies caused by the War on Terror and media portrayals is partly so strong because Islam isn't geopolitically confined in the same way the Cold War was. When 9/11 happened, the US and the UK invaded Afghanistan and Iraq, but the "enemy" doesn't live in one place, but rather in an imagination, an imaginary landscape. That's what makes all people of colour vulnerable to Islamophobic racism. We all become targets under the War on Terror.

Terror perpetuates terror. We've seen this in the way our own communities interact with each other across faith lines. It's not just white people who have underlying negative feelings about Muslims—many people of colour also do.

When Assata Shakur was placed on the FBI's 10 Most Wanted List, she was the only woman on the list. This was no coincidence. Ideas of blackness are reworked and Otherness expanded to continue anti-blackness in new ways. While Assata isn't Muslim, her name certainly is read as a Muslim name. Islamophobia is a dual attack on black communities in the US because of the long-standing history of radical Black Islam in the United States, with advocates such as Muhammad Ali and Malcolm X. In the case of Shakur, traditional forms of bigotry against people of African descent becomes entwined with a new and political faith-based hatred. These are some of the new ways that Islamophobia effects all of us: even those who aren't Muslim.

As a person of colour, it's easier to spot discrimination or racism based solely on colour or ethnicity but maybe not so easy to spot racism based on religion. Conversations about racisms—for example, race or Islamophobia—are often quite similar to each other. We often hear that you can't be racist towards Muslims because Muslims aren't a race, but that's not the case when

Muslims are predominantly people of colour and Islam is racialised. However, it's hard to know what to say to such disarming comments.

The solution for combating Islamophobia is to build support for people of colour. Islam is incredibly diverse and always has been. Our equation of Islam with the Middle East is driven by our governments, as opposed to a wider understanding of the Muslim world. One very tangible thing we can do is take time to educate ourselves on Islam to be better placed and prepared for these conversations. For example, I've routinely heard "shariah law wants to kill gay people" used as a way to normalise anti-Muslim discussions. These conversations do not acknowledge that there are gay Muslims, or that the wars in Iraq and Afghanistan certainly killed queer Muslims of colour. Another example is the idea that Muslim women "need" to be saved from the men. Any conversation in this vein should naturally cross over with discussions of intersectional feminism. Why do women of colour need to be "saved" by predominantly European saviours, either through bombing Muslim countries or through methods as violent as pulling off hijabs?

Educating ourselves can be as easy as a quick Google search or walking into a mosque if you live in a town or city that's large enough to have one. Self-education allows non-Muslims to talk about Islam and debunk common myths, but also to consciousness-raise with other people of colour. This means that Muslims don't have to keep having the same conversations with people.

Islam has a really varied and progressive history, one that is currently being forgotten as we battle with bigots on their terms.

Self-education and the support of others' education forges solidarity during these tenuous times.

I've got friends who have told me that they have allowed Islamophobic or racially charged comments to remain unchallenged for their own comfort. As PoC, we have more to lose in the stakes of these conversations. Treat Islamophobic comments as you would ideally treat any racist comments: call it out and treat it with zero tolerance.

Yasmin Begum *is a Pakistani-Welsh writer and activist from Wales, United Kingdom. Yasmin is a graduate from the* School of Oriental and African Studies, University of London. *She is interested in religion, feminism and decolonial theory.*

How Telling Each Other To "Google It" Hurts Our Movements

by Princess Harmony Rodriguez

Many of us have had the privilege of access to educational tools to learn about ourselves, our histories and/or our positions in society. As knowledge becomes more available in new ways through technology, it can be easy to forget that there are still many of us who are not able to reap the benefits.

I have noticed that we can be quick to dismiss questions in activist spaces. Instead of helping each other, we often tell folks to "Google it" on their own time. Looking up a concept on Google is not available to everyone. For reasons of class, disability, and educational privilege, we need to be wary of answering people's questions by telling them to just look it up themselves.

Of course, there are times that saying something like "Google it" protects us from having to offer unpaid teaching moments to people who hold privilege over us. These people ask us to teach them about oppression as a way to demand labor and to derail conversations, and in that context, telling them to consult

Google is completely okay.

That said, we need to rethink telling people in our own communities, people whose participation we need in our movements, to just go learn these concepts for themselves, especially when these are people who we hold privilege over.

I want us to aim to be as helpful as we can in ways that serve all of us instead of deferring important questions in our communities to Google searches.

Here's a few reasons why "Google it" and similar sentiments aren't always the best response to questions.

1. People may need more support

I once told a person to "Google it" without knowing that they had reading issues. I had unknowingly perpetuated ableism by assuming they learned best by reading.

At the core of the "learn it on your own" philosophy stands the ableist assumption that everyone can learn by reading on their own and that's simply not the case. Mental illnesses such as depression, certain learning disabilities, and disabilities affecting memory can make learning abstract concepts difficult and perhaps even impossible.

In many activist spaces we talk about centering those most affected by oppression but isn't it contradictory that we tell those very folks to figure out things on their own?

Those who are neurotypical hold privilege over those of

us who are neurodivergent. The way that many revolutionary spaces are run erases neurodivergent people. Rather than finding multiple ways to communicate ideas, these spaces rely on the written word. As members of various social justice movements, we need to remember that to create a more accessible movement means recognizing that learning doesn't happen the same way for everyone.

2. Barriers to academic language

There are many academic works that form the basis for our current understandings of liberation in activist spaces, such as the concepts of intersectionality, social construction, and privilege.

Often, these concepts are written about at a graduate school reading level. Many academic books about trans liberation are totally inaccessible to trans people because of many barriers for us to receive higher education, such as high tuition rates and discrimination.

When I was trying to learn about ideas such as gender performativity, I had the privilege of being taught by other trans people. If someone had told me to "Google it" instead, I'd have been lost and completely unable to understand it.

I learn best through conversations when I can share my own experiences and connect them to struggles of other people. I've had conversations on Twitter and Facebook that were really helpful for understanding and applying new concepts.

When we say "read a book" to someone in our community who asks a question, especially when they don't understand the academic language being used, we block them out of conversations where their input is critical.

Even at times when we cannot give personal responses to each other's questions, there are countless YouTube vloggers who talk about social justice concepts, whose videos are great resources to show to people.

3. Inaccessible resources

Even in our revolutionary spaces, we replicate the very systems we aim to fight when we tell folks to figure out answers to their questions on their own.

Rural areas often lack the infrastructure to provide the Internet that some of us enjoy and rely upon to learn revolutionary theories. In the United States, there remain many homes without an internet service subscription. For example, only 57% of black households have access to the internet at home. And there exist even more homes, often in rural areas, without access to quality internet. In order to reach Google, there has to first be working Internet or data connection.

While I experience oppression for being afrolatin and trans, I also have the privileges of access to higher education and high-quality internet. I want to move away from telling folks without that access to "Google it" if they asked me a question.

4. Liberation is collective, not individual

In order to uplift ourselves, we have to uplift all of us. We cannot educate ourselves about liberation and consider our work done. Concepts of liberation need to be available to everyone in our community who wants access and not just those of us who learn by reading Google search results. This requires a willingness on our part to make a point of helping each other beyond deferring to Google searches to teach us.

Whether it's linking to videos or specific pieces, personally talking to people, or communicating it through art, there are alternate ways of teaching each other without resorting to "Google it."

Realistically, we can only do what we have the energy to do, but we should still make a point to help each other, so we can all go on and share what we learn with even more people in our communities.

I want to see a world where everyone is free. Everyone reading this should want that, too.

Princess Harmony Rodriguez is unapologetic afrolatin weeb trash that likes anime, visual novels, and video games. Her favorite snack is Strawberry Pocky and she loves empanadas. Oh, and she likes shiny things. Especially glittery shiny things.

The Safe Word Is Lemonade

by Francesca Walker

The safe word is lemonade because although Beyoncé does not represent this fat, Black femme in her visual album, she does manage to encapsulate the depths of Black women's pain and generational trauma in an hour. In a single album, she exposes our suffering for what it is and reveals that oftentimes the perpetrator can be someone we deeply love. She shows the profundity of a Black woman's love and the rage that can ensue when we make the decision to no longer consent to being disregarded, despite that love. The safe word is necessary so they know when they have gone further than I am ready to go in any given moment—they, in this case, being non-Black people of color.

I have not been in very many romantic relationships but there have been a few meaningful ones. The most recent, with an Indo-Guyanese person, ended with him on my blocked caller list and resentment on my part—not just towards him, but towards all non-Black people of color.

In almost every relationship I have been in, dishonesty and

deception reared their ugly heads, which planted the seed for trust issues. My relationship to this brown man was the only relationship I have been in where I truly felt that our love and commitment to each other was mutual and unconditional. In fact, this was the only relationship that I have ever had that I felt compelled to disclose to my mother. There was no room or desire for dishonesty or deception. Sure, there were disagreements, but when it was all said and done, we always brought it back to the love and kept it moving from there.

As the relationship became more serious, he was also eager to tell his family about it. They were excited to hear that he had found someone and wanted to know more about the mystery woman. However, once he showed them a picture of me, their reactions transformed from intrigue to disappointment. The first words they uttered were, "are you serious?" followed by, "she's Black." Clearly upset, my then-boyfriend left the house so that he could recount the interaction with me over the phone. During this time, he received several phone calls from various members of his family telling him how disappointed they were in him and how this great shame—that shame being me—was upsetting his mother. Even though they told him that their dismissal of me was simply a desire to "keep it in the culture," what they were really conveying was that they did not want someone like me, a Black woman, to be a part of their family. Later on that day, I received a call from my then-boyfriend telling me, in essence, that his fear of disappointing his family was greater than his love for me and that it was over. Shortly after, he became blocked caller number 12 and, in the process, I ended up blocking the entire non-Black people of color community.

I was deeply hurt by this rejection I had experienced on account of this brown man and his devout Christian family. They despised the idea of me. I began to slip back into old habits and despise myself, but this time felt different. The truth is, it was not their anti-Black sentiment alone that got to me. I am convinced that if they were a white family (which I would never date into because homie don't play that), it would not breed self-loathing. It would not breed this new form of self-hatred where I found myself flirting with the idea of suicide. I realized that I was hurt because I was prepared to embrace them, wholeheartedly, into my family. I was hurt because my imagination of several Afro-Panamanian/Indo-Guyanese family gatherings full of love and community had been shattered. This particular moment of rejection gave birth to my resentment, not simply towards this brown family, but towards all non-Black people of color. My personal resentment, in addition to public incidents of violence such as the murder of Akai Gurley at the hands of Peter Liang, added potency to the poison that was already coursing through my veins—like some bitter ass lemonade.

My resentment towards non-Black people of color was and continues to be a coping mechanism—a way to ensure they do not have the power or opportunity to destroy me in a way that could have tragically been successful. Then there are the rare moments when I stumble upon things such as the Committee Against Anti-Asian Violence (CAAAV) and their joint statement with other AAPI organizations demanding justice for the murder of Akai Gurley and standing in their convictions, even as they receive threats and harassment from some anti-Black members of Chinese and larger Asian American communities. In moments like these where I see non-Black people of color resisting anti-Black racism and truly exemplifying people of color solidarity, my resentment becomes slightly diluted and my finger begins to hover over the unblock caller button for about two seconds, but then *lemonade.*

This essay of acknowledgment is my first step into the healing process and I believe that an authentic people of color community, where solidarity resists anti-Black racism, is action-oriented, and is rooted in genuine love is integral to that process. Non-Black people of color: my fat, Black femme lemonade is still bitter as fuck, but it is your responsibility to reach out and repair the damage you have done. The hope is that one day I will trust you again. One day, I will believe you when you say you love me and will not be afraid to outwardly reciprocate that love. One day, I will not scoff at the notion of people of color solidarity and not feel the need to pull out my safe word because you are trying to embrace me in a way that I am not ready to be embraced by you yet. Until then, you are going to have to keep that sugar coming until my lemonade is ready to be enjoyed in community with you.

Francesca E. Walker is a Black Panamanian American queer woman born and raised in the heart of Brooklyn, NY. When she's not working in higher education administration, you can find her supporting anti-gentrification community organizing and reminding hotep Black men that Black women and Black queer people are magical.

Uprisings and Solidarity:
How Unity Is Informed By Community

by Patrisse Cullors

I grew up in the San Fernando Valley, a suburb of Los Angeles. Los Angeles County is more than fifty percent Latino, and my neighborhood was reflective of that, as were my relationships and cultural experiences. In fact, some of my first caregivers were Mexican-American, domestic workers who cared for me as well as they did their kids.

I learned to speak Spanish, learned traditional Mexican Folklorico dancing, and throughout elementary school I was almost always the only non-Latina girl in class. Although I am not Mexican, I was immersed in Mexican culture, and it felt a lot like home.

In 1992, amidst the uprising in Los Angeles after the brutal beating of Rodney King, the media reported time and again that Black and Latino communities were at odds. Our local news station would show images of Black and Latino people fighting one another. They would focus on "gang violence" and blast messages through the TV screen about how our people were drug users and uneducated. It wasn't a narrative I saw playing out in my neighborhood, so I was surprised when one day during recess a fight erupted between me and my Black and Latino classmates.

The fight involved us enacting what we had been seeing on news stations. We literally were mimicking verbatim what we had seen on the screen. At one point, I remember yelling out the famous words, 'Somebody help this man," uttered by a good Samaritan who witnessed the beating of Reginald Denny. It felt strange, that we, children, would play out such violence in our school settings, that part of how we were trying to understand the reality of the uprisings was through copying what we saw. The news was telling a politicized story about us, one that we bought into and one that stripped us of our collective dignity. We didn't have to fight each other, but children often practice the behaviors they see around them. Our mocking of the uprisings was a painful attempt at processing the repetitive violence issued out by mainstream media.

The fight landed many of us in the assistant principal's office. She was a thin-framed, Black woman who wore purple and had classic feathered hair. She sat us down and made us discuss why were fighting each other. None of us had a good enough answer, but we did discuss what the media called "the riots." One by one we told our assistant principal how frightened we were by the uprisings. We explained how we were afraid we would be hurt by the people who were in the uprisings. We cried a lot. She looked at each of us gently, told us she had an assignment for us, wrote it on a piece of paper and made each of us read it aloud.

We were asked to team up. If you were Black, you had to team up with someone Latino and vice versa. She told us to learn about one another and to tell each other stories about our lives and experiences. In addition, she asked us to research where each other came from and prominent figures from each other's communities. The final request was for us to start playing basketball together, and we were instructed to do so for the remainder of the school year.

We did as we were told. I sat with Richie, short for Ricardo, and shared the rich history I learned about Mexico, specifically Jalisco. Jalisco, a western state off the Pacific Ocean, where mariachi music was started. He talked about the African-American influence on America. Both of us felt impressed with each other. I was eight and he was nine, and I learned the value of being in community and actually knowing the community you are a part of. I learned the value of community research. The moment I learned Richie's heritage, I felt closer to him and the community I was being raised around.

It has been more than 20 years and I am an organizer in the same community in which I grew up. It looks the same and different now. Working across communities to support the empowerment of people color, I realize how profoundly important my assistant principal's actions were. She created and developed an environment where Black and Latino kids could learn about how our differences actually enhance how we can be in solidarity with one another. I was able to have compassion for Richie's family as I learned about the country his parents immigrated from. I learned about the specific hardships that forced his family out of Mexico and into Los Angeles. These struggles were not the same as my family's, but reminded me of how violent racism pushed my family out of the south. Mine and Richie's migration stories were different but allowed for a new understanding of unity.

Our assistant principal knew better than we that there are systems meant to divide us, systems that urge us to see our struggles as inherently different. And while I recognize our unique differences, we share experiences that bind us and that make it increasingly more important that we work together. Now is the time to be the most unapologetic in our move towards solidarity with each other. Solidarity doesn't equate erasing our differences. It actually pushes us to learn and understand our differences. We must use our differences as a platform for greater unity. Let us show up for each other in all the ways that are possible and that honor our struggles and our triumphs.

Patrisse Cullors is an artist, organizer, and freedom fighter from LA. Co-founder of Black Lives Matter, she is also a performance artist, Fulbright scholar, public speaker, and an NAACP History Maker. She was named by the Los Angeles Times as a Civil Rights Leader for the 21st Century.

It's Time to Destroy Anti-Blackness in the Sikh Community

by Kanwalroop Kaur Singh

Initially after Michael Brown's death, I argued intensely with my family for hours, trying to convince them that "violent" protest was not only justified, but necessary in the wake of the white supremacist state's unabashed murder of black people. They countered with a variety of racist and anti-black statements, ranging from describing black bodies as violent, to claiming that the black community should be "satisfied" with the rights that it had. I couldn't comprehend it. My (mostly immigrant) family had firsthand experience with police brutality and racism in India and in the U.S., as did my uncles, my extended family, and in fact, almost ALL of my community, so why the inability to comprehend the intersection of our struggles?

As many other Sikhs have, I have grown up seeing temple walls lined with the photos of our martyrs, many of whom were murdered by police at a time when being a "Sikh" was perceived as being a "violent terrorist." This continues today in both the U.S. and Canada, resulting most recently in the cold-blooded massacre of 6 Sikhs within a temple by a white supremacist but also numerous accounts of assault, murder, and bullying outside of our places of worship, and in our daily lives.

We are a "minority" in any country we go to, but perhaps most strongly in India, where we are actually most numerous. Due to the inseparable combination of Hindu dominance (a legacy of colonial dominance) and the construction of the oppressive nation-state, Sikhs in India are reduced to unthinking, primitive buffoons in Bollywood films; are faced with repeated violent physical attacks by Hindu nationalists; are drowning in high rates of drug addiction; and have been murdered in the thousands by the Indian state since 1984.

Even our arrival in the U.S. near the turn of the 20th century was laced with the discrimination of the Alien Land Law, and the Asiatic Barred Zone Act, among others, in addition to whole segments of our community being beaten and run out of white towns in race riots started by white supremacists. Joan Jensen, in her book, Passage From India, cites historical accounts of white men occupying positions in the power structure calling Sikhs the n-word, or calling them "black," barring them from eating at white restaurants, and exercising overt wage-based discrimination against them. Yet despite this racism, Sikhs in America, such as Bhagat Singh Thind, still tried to assimilate to the white norm by fighting for the legal right to be recognized as white due to trumped up and mostly baseless connections with a distant "Aryan race." This perhaps reveals how the differences in the racialization of Sikh and Black communities allowed Sikhs to be placed higher on the white supremacist scale of racial hierarchy. Sikhs were still able to benefit from white supremacy. Our racialization was not destructive to our community to the same extent that the black community's was and continues to be.

Given the fact that most of the worlds nation-states/empires and their "law enforcement" agents have literally murdered or endorsed the murder of Sikhs, it was heartbreaking to me that my parents, being the people who taught me my history, could not see the importance, let alone be in solidarity with, the powerful black struggle against injustice rising around the country. But I realized something the minute my dad said, "if Sikhs had been able to get half as much national media attention as the Ferguson struggle was getting for one of our murdered sons, then we would have been satisfied." I realized then that the flaw in my dad's thinking, and that of many others in our community, was that he was unable to comprehend the notion of interracial/intercommunal solidarity between oppressed peoples. He grew up in a country where the downtrodden did not draw strength from each other's struggles, but rather were pitted, and thus pitted themselves, against the very communities that they should have been aligned with—the other communities that had been violated by the Indian state (Dalits, Muslims, Christians, queers, non-elite women, etc.). He saw the struggle of marginalized communities as taking place in a competitive arena, where each community had to prove to the oppressor that they were the most oppressed and beg the oppressor to integrate them into the power structure, instead of seeing struggle as collective, as taking place at a communal gathering where communities could bond with each other, draw from the differences and similarities of their struggles to overturn a power structure.

He was busy playing oppression Olympics, thinking that we had to compete with other communities that were being systematically eliminated, instead of forge our struggles collectively and be willing to make huge sacrifices for each other in the name of genuine solidarity. In fact, he was jealous. Because black Americans' ability to mobilize collectively around injustice, accurately name the violence committed against them, set up memorials, establish organizations, and write and publish accounts of their own history is truly phenomenal. This is a role model for resistance, a fucking guide. Perhaps this is what he wishes we could have accomplished in what is often seen as a "tragic" history.

I wish it, too. But in order for this to happen, the Sikh community must be a consistently mobilized contingent that represents itself at black struggles around the country and around the world. Sikhs must figuratively and physically be part of the black struggle, wherever it needs us to be. Only then will we be able to learn from this beautiful community, and only then will the black community partake in Sikh struggles against injustice, when the need arises. Perhaps most importantly, though, the anti-blackness that floods through our homes needs to be actively destroyed at the same time that we go outside of our homes and declare solidarity with the black struggle.

Kanwalroop Kaur Singh is an aspiring Sikh writer and activist-scholar. Her name means "form of a lotus" in Punjabi. Daughter of immigrants, she was born in California but her roots lie in both the Pakistan and India sides of modern-day Punjab.

POC Solidarity In Love
How To Support Our Black Partners and Friends In These Trying Times
by CarmenLeah Ascencio

I am a non-Black Latina partnered with a Black woman. The night Michael Brown was murdered by Darren Wilson in Ferguson, my partner was glued to her Twitter account, raising her voice about the injustice, conversing with other black people, and poring over the news. At the time, she and I had an ongoing conflict about her Twitter addiction. Late into the evening, when I saw that she was still on Twitter, I became annoyed and asked when she was going to get offline. After some disagreement, she burst into tears. She expressed deep upset at my lack of consideration for her need to be in connection with other Black people at that moment. ¡Ay, que pendeja yo fui! I was centering my feelings over her very real experiences of oppression, adding to her distress and denying her the support she needed at such an enraging and painful time. And that, my non-Black POC friends, isn't what POC solidarity in love looks like.

Non-black POC in relationships with Black people have a responsibility to figure out the best way to act in solidarity with our partners and friends. This responsibility shouldn't be work, but rather an effort arising from love. If we aren't down to figure this out, then we shouldn't get involved with Black folks who are already taking a risk in loving someone who does not understand what it's like to live with the often-dangerous reality of being Black (and queer or trans) in this country.

To help us all out, including myself, I've compiled a short list of some basic places to start as non-Black POC trying to act in solidarity and provide support to the Black people we are in relationships with.

1. Offer concrete support and take care. When shit is going down and your partner or friend is hurting because of things like police brutality against Black people, ask what you can do for them. If they aren't sure, start with the simple acts of caring. Cook for them, run errands they're too upset or pre-occupied to do, massage their shoulders, buy their favorite treat—whatever caring acts you can think of so your partner or friend can focus on getting the support they need and organizing whatever action they might want to take.

2. Acknowledge when you fuck up and don't do it again. You're probably gonna mess up at least once when it comes to missing something important as a non-Black POC in a relationship with a Black person. When your partner or friend tells you that you messed up or don't understand something pertaining to their

racial experience, don't get defensive and give a bunch of justifications for your mistake. Listen to them and own your error. More importantly, don't do it again. Acknowledging you messed up isn't worth much if you don't change your behavior. After the Twitter Incident with my partner, I apologized, understood why centering my feelings right then wasn't cool, and have not made the mistake again.

3. Don't make it about you when it isn't. Don't get your feelings hurt if your partner or friend doesn't want to share and be vulnerable with you about the pain they experience related to living with the legacy and current reality of being Black in the U.S. After watching *12 Years A Slave*, although we both were in tears, my partner's tears were from a different experience than mine. As much as I wanted to comfort her, she expressed the need to have that kind of experience with other Black people. Of course. Makes total sense and that need didn't have anything to do with me.

4. Give time and space. Know that your partner or friend may need their own time and space with other Black folks without you, especially when it comes to discussing the oppression Black people face (but not only then). Make sure to be supportive and understanding of this. Never make this important time difficult for them to have.

5. Engage from a place of not knowing. As much as non-Black POC might think we understand, we don't experience racism in the same ways Black people do. As enraging as police brutality against Black people is to me, I do not experience this rage the same way my partner does. I cannot, because I have no idea what it is like to be Black. Discuss anti-black oppression from the stance that you don't know in the same way your partner or friend does. Listen carefully without assuming you know what they are talking about. As their partner and primary support, or their close friend, you should never be someone they experience frustration with when speaking about their experience as a Black person.

6. If you do activist work together, step back if the issue pertains to anti-black oppression. Don't hold the megaphone, don't be at the front of the march (unless you're asked to be there), don't speak more than they do, don't act like anti-black oppression is the same as the oppression you face as a non-Black POC, and stay home if they want to organize Black-only direct actions. Ask how you can play a supportive role and check in to make sure any actions you take independently are helpful to them.

7. Remember you still benefit from anti-blackness. Even though you love your partner or friend, you still benefit from and are complicit in anti-blackness. Take action to push back against the privilege you have because of this. For example, maybe you

want your partner to come to your majority white or non-black POC work party, social gathering or family event, but they feel uncomfortable in a setting without any other Black people, especially right now. Think about the lack of discomfort you might feel in these spaces due to your non-black race privilege, understand your partner's needs and be ok with them sitting certain events out regardless of how much you want their company.

8. Understand that you don't get a pass. Dating/loving/partnering with a Black person doesn't get you off the hook on examining and doing something about anti-blackness, including your own. Yes, you can be with a Black person and have Black friends and still hold anti-black ideas. Being with a Black person doesn't absolve you from doing the work to understand and challenge anti-black oppression, in yourself and in the world.

This is not a comprehensive list, but are some basic actions that non-Black POC can take to be in solidarity with our Black partners and friends; not just for the struggle, but for the health and well-being of the people we love. ¡Pa'Lante!

CarmenLeah Ascencio *is a public health social worker, community theatre facilitator, trauma-sensitive yoga instructor, educator and proud Boricua 2nd generation queer femme. She is the director of* Get Free *and the creator of* Freedom Labor Love. *She speaks and facilitates* BGD Get Free *workshops at organizations and schools.*

7 Ways to Turn Your Anger Over Sandra Bland Into Action In Support of Incarcerated (and Formerly Incarcerated) Black Women

by Desiree Stevens

The funneling of black children through the school-to-prison pipeline is a dangerous trend that pervades society. As a result, black people make up a disproportionately high percentage of the prison population. For young black girls, the reality is that we make the largest growing demographic of incarcerated people in the U.S.

With #BlackLivesMatter rallies occurring across the nation, and tragic stories such as those of Natasha McKenna and Sandra Bland surfacing every week, it's important now more than ever to center the experiences of formerly and currently incarcerated black women. It's crucial to acknowledge and amplify our voices if we wish to have a truly inclusive and liberating movement.

I have always been outspoken about my views regarding white supremacy and anti-black racism. The predominately white university I attended had a history of putting on minstrel shows, further marginalizing the already small black student body. I was hanging with friends one night and race was brought up. Feeling triggered, our conversation quickly escalated into a heated debate. Next I recall being pepper-sprayed, slammed against a police car, and without my rights read to me, unfairly taken to jail. While behind bars, I was mistreated and neglected. I experienced physical abuse by correctional officers, who hurled misogynoiristic slurs at me. Even after release, I still carry the trauma. Many black women will continue to live through these conditions, with some, like Natasha McKenna and Sandra Bland, even dying at the hands of our captors. If we really believe that black lives matter, we must actively take steps to show up for black women.

There are ways we can start today:

1. Let us live. The criminalization of black girls starts early; they face higher rates of suspension compared to their non-black counterparts, which begins and upholds the school to prison pipeline. Showing up for incarcerated black women means allowing space for us to live authentically. We live in a heightened state of being policed but our personal treatment of black girls can make a difference. Support our agency. Let us dance. Let us wear our hair in a way we see fit. Support us in taking back our autonomy in a proactive way.

2. De-stigmatize your perception of incarceration. In a criminal (in)justice system that was built on criminalizing black

people, where prosecutors are ninety-five percent white, and where jurors are overwhelmingly white, it's no surprise that black people face harsher and longer sentences. From Jim Crow to the "War on Drugs," the livelihood of black people has been and continues to be policed. As black women, our actions, like grocery shopping, walking to a bar as a black trans woman, or defending ourselves against domestic violence, carry the risk of incarceration or death. In an effort to fight for black women and femmes who are disproportionately targeted by these laws, it's important to realize how we are systematically policed and how that manifests into imprisonment.

3. Uplift the narratives of incarcerated black women. In the US, black women are more likely to face imprisonment than women of any other racial group, yet mainstream media ignores our stories. It's important to bring our narratives to light. Black women's experiences with police brutality, mistreatment inside prison, and unfair sentencing need to be shared. Fundraise for our attendance to statewide and national conferences so we have a greater platform to share our truths. #SayOurNames. Share our stories. Center us, and let it be known that #IncarceratedBlackWomensLivesMatter, too.

4. Intentionally give space. There is a lot of pain associated

with being institutionalized and carrying the risk of incarceration. Since our voices are often silenced, it's important for us to have a space to go to where we are heard and feel validated. Be that space.

5. Work with orgs that serve incarcerated people and center black women & femmes. Despite constant harassment on the inside, one of the most important experiences I had was a phone call from my sibling. It kept me going and gave me something to live for. Being locked up can be bleak but it doesn't have to be. Black & Pink and Dignity & Power Now are just two entities that offer support to currently and formerly incarcerated people. Be intentional about providing support to black queer and trans women, as we often deal with intersectional forms of violence in and out of institutions. Write a letter, make a phone call, put some money on our books; small things like this can be hugely impactful for us, and can make time spent on the inside a little less dreadful.

6. Share the wealth! It can be difficult to navigate life once released from jail. With a criminal record, it can be difficult and nearly impossible to secure employment. Monetary assistance is essential. Donate to crowdfunding efforts that help once-jailed black women in our re-entry efforts. Sup-

port the entrepreneurial projects of formerly incarcerated black women. If you cannot give money directly, consider donating items to community centers that focus on giving back to black women. Contributions like this can drastically change the life of a black women whose life is forever changed because of incarceration.

7. Advocate for and support policy changes. There is legislation in place that unfairly criminalizes black women and you can play a role in eliminating it. For example, the zero-tolerance policies that exist in primary and secondary schools disproportionately target young black girls at our most vulnerable phase of development and need to be abolished. An alternative response could be restorative justice, a community-based response to conflict. This method minimizes the influence of police and offers all parties involved the opportunity to be accountable. At the same time, it allows young black girls the safety from having to interact with oppressive police officers. Implementing these can be instrumental in creating change. President Obama just unveiled new criminal justice proposals to lessen the impact of mass incarceration in the US. These include minimizing sentences for nonviolent drug possession, eliminating solitary confinement, "banning the box" on job applications, and restoring voting rights to released prisoners. We also need to support these reforms and fight to abolish other harmful laws.

In the midst of anti-black misogyny, and the subsequent criminalization that black women and girls are subject to, it's our collective duty to memorialize those we've lost at the hands of our oppressors and to show up for black women and girls who continue to be subjected to them. Together, we can help shift the narratives of incarcerated black women.

Desiree Stevens *has a passion for music, dismantling white supremacy, & all snacks labeled flamin' hot. She was honored for her work by the* National Black Justice Coalition.

Dreaming Forward

by Jackie Fawn

Jackie Fawn *uses her art to create stories through her illustrations focused on indigenous, social, and environmental issues.*
- Yurok, Washoe, Filipina

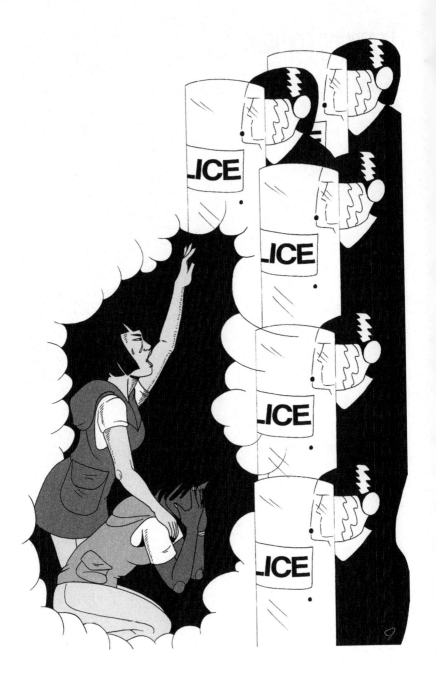

JACKIE FAWN

JACKIE FAWN

To Be Diné, To Be Me
Engaging with Solidarity
by Charlie Scott

Yá'át'ééh, shí éí Charlie Scott yinishyé. Naasht'ézhí Tábaahá nishłí, Tsénjíkiní báshíshchíín, Áshįįhí dashicheii, dóó Kiis'áanii dashinalí. Ch'ínílį´déé naashá.

Hello, I am named Charlie Scott. I am of the Zuni Water Edge Clan, born for the Honeycomb Rock People of the Cliff Dwellers People Clan, my maternal grandfathers are of the Salt People Clan, and my paternal grandfathers are of the Hopi Sun Clan. By this traditional introduction, I am showing you who I am, who my relatives are, and who I represent.

I was born and raised in Chinle, Arizona. I attended kindergarten in the Chinle Unified School district, and subsequently 1st, 2nd, 3rd, all the way to graduating in 2013 from Chinle High School. My whole educational career revolved around me living and learning on the Navajo Nation.

Growing up on my reservation, racism was foreign to me. I did not understand the sort of marginalization that came when one is not identified or perceived as white. I was taught about the cultural genocide and the forced gathering and trapping of my people at Fort Sumner/Bosque Redondo, which is known to us as the Long Walk. Even though historical events were taught to me, all I saw around me was my people in positions of power and survival. We had our own government, in which our president has to speak Diné bizaad fluently. Our Miss Navajo has to be able to butcher a sheep and speak Diné bizaad fluently, too.

I knew that people were different from me because they were not Navajo or Diné. Within the schools that I attended, I only knew of one or two fully white students. Most of the other students were multiracial. Some were Bilagáana (white) and Diné, Naakai Dine'é (Mexican, Hispanic, or Latinx) and Diné, or Diné and another Indigenous community. There is such an emphasis on our language, our culture, and our heritage that I barely noticed or was conscious of the emphasis on skin and the differences of living and existing off of the Navajo Nation.

During my first year at Brown University, I struggled with what it meant to be Navajo, to be Diné, to be an Indigenous person within the United States. I was taught that education was a ladder to success. That I was meant to climb that ladder and to care, to love, and to fight for my family because I was the future for them. I arrived at Brown with these teachings, believing that I only needed my family and my education to thrive. At Brown, I became very aware of how my racial identity is consistently and constantly regulated and read. Every single time I am off of the Navajo Nation, non-Diné people speak to me in Spanish and I am confused for a moment. I tell them that I do not speak Spanish, nor am I Latinx. Their first response is "Are you sure?" or "Oh, then what are you?"

Within my first few months at Brown, then-New York City police commissioner Ray Kelly was invited to campus to provide a lecture titled, "Proactive Policing in America's Biggest City". In response, around 100 students and community members gathered outside the List Art Center an hour before the lecture was scheduled to start, chanting phrases such as, "Ray Kelly, you can't hide, we charge you with homicide" and holding signs with phrases like, "Stop police brutality", "Brown is complicit" and "Ray(cist) Kelly".

I was torn between arguments for challenging systemic racism and arguments for freedom of speech. I was torn between friends. These divisions caused me mental stress because I did not know who to side with, and there was pressure on both sides to choose.

It was during this time that I had the most difficulty accepting that racism existed. I was interacting with racial minorities for the first time and filtering those interactions through a racial lens. I felt uncomfortable around dark-skinned black people. I avoided interacting with Latinx people because I did not want to be mistaken for one, and the same for Asian people. I interpreted through stereotypes, rather than debunking and challenging what I was taught. I was not aware of these judgments that I was making and how much I was isolating myself from people. I kept myself from interacting with people and caring for people because of my lack of knowledge of race and racism.

I did not know what it meant to be a person of color because I had never identified as a person of color or as a racial minority. I refused to acknowledge that racism existed because I thought I was empowered in knowing who I was and being in control of people's perception of me.

Following the Ray Kelly protest, I made myself attend the series of difficult conversations that were held by the administrators of Brown University in the next couple of days. It was at these spaces that I was able to get a grasp of how racism operated within the justice system, and within the larger social systems of the United States. It caused me to reevaluate how I saw myself within the Brown University community and my own community.

After my first, tough year at Brown, being on the Navajo Nation was difficult for me. I became aware of how much race and racism was an integral part of my community. The reactions and interactions that I have seen in my community—moments of awkward silence when the only black family shops and dines; the openness of the smiling waitress or cashier to white tourists, and the looks of annoyance towards the Asian tourists. It took me leaving my community and attending a school far away to recognize and understand the reactions that racism produced.

I knew that I was Diné, Hopi, Yavapai and Zuni. I was never a Native American or an American Indian, those words never suited me, and even now I have some resistance to being called an Indigenous person, yet I accept that title because the conversations on Indigenous identity are difficult and complex, as are any conversations on racial identities.

I ask myself every single day how can I, as a racialized, queer, gender non-binary person of color promote and maintain solidarity with other people of color? How can I achieve my mother's and ancestors' dream for me to thrive and succeed without stepping on someone's hand, foot, or head to get there?

In my peoples' language and culture, we are told to follow two teachings, the Blessing Way and the Protection Way. There are twenty-eight values in total and all advise us, the Diné, of how we are supposed to live our lives in hopes to find hózhó or, in English, balance and harmony. When I conceptualize solidarity, I think of ajooba'—to care, a'yóó'óní—to love, and k'ézhnídzin—to value your kin and familial relations. Ajooba', a'yóó'óní, dóó k'ézhnídzin are easier to do with the people I know and grew up with but difficult to follow with non-Indigenous people of color because it requires me to rethink how I navigate my life. Solidarity for me as a multiracial Indigenous person is difficult to conceptualize because it requires me to sacrifice something that my parents and ancestors wanted me to have.

My ancestors were not brought here as enslaved peoples to build an empire over the dead bodies of millions of Indigenous peoples. My family does not have to cross borders and obtain citizenship within the United States. Instead, my family and my community has a different struggle. As Indigenous peoples of the United States, which is comprised of different Indigenous communities with different cultures and traditions, we have a unique experience that is based upon treaties and agreements with European-settlers and my ancestors. I have difficulty with envisioning solidarity because I fear what that means for my people who have relied upon these treaties for centuries and have built their communities around them. My ancestors have given up their land and life in hopes that their children and their children's children would be given a fighting chance to survive and thrive. Being a multiracial Indigenous person in the United States is a double-edged sword. On one side, I have the privilege of belonging and living on my ancestral home. On the other side, my community and other Indigenous communities have become forced to live in third-world conditions with very little running water or electricity, and forced to live in a bounded area of land. Our liberation requires the return of Indigenous land and life, yet it is that liberation that has me hesitating. If, we, Indigenous peoples, were to regain our land and life, it allows us to make our roots stronger than ever, yet it could also mean the dispossession and the forced removal of non-Indigenous people of color within the United States.

I hesitate because of what it that could mean for non-Indigenous people of color here. They are, intentionally or not, complicit in maintaining the suppression of the return of Indigenous land and life. Yet, they also may not have an ancestral home to go back to or be able to regain because of the forced enslavement of black people and the forced migration of those who were affected by the globalizing policies of the United States. This is what has me hesitating in wanting my land to be returned to me.

I believe that solidarity with Indigenous peoples of the United States requires a recognition of how intertwined solidarity has become in maintaining the loss of Indigenous land, yet for Indigenous peoples to gain solidarity requires us to recognize how complicit we have become in isolating ourselves from participating in any sort of major movements for people outside of our communities.

My perception of caring, loving, and family—ajooba', a'yóó'óní, dóó k'ézhnídzin—were very narrow. I did not think that racism affected me. I did not think that I was involved or complicit in racism. But I am.

I think one of the greatest things about being at Brown and being able to travel off the Navajo Nation is that I am interacting with people who I have come to know and care for. It is because of them and their passions that I choose to create and foster solidarity. I have become hopeful about my capacity to care, love and value my friendships my community, and my family.

Charlie Scott is a multiracial indigenous scholar from the Navajo Nation. With their traditional moccasins on, they are on the path of re-discovering queer indigeneity and reclaiming the medium of photography for empowering Indigenous youth. They're still learning ways to be accessible and compassionate alongside a community with trauma and resilience.

Disabling the QTPoC Future

by Ngọc Loan Trân

When I started exploring what queerness meant to me, I was obsessed with my body. I was obsessed with learning how it could look, feel, taste, and *be* next to a body that looked like mine, a queer body just like mine, a queer body of color just like mine. I spent a lot of time imagining more comfort in intimacy, in desire, in community. And when I could finally experience it, I was grateful for the communities that welcomed me in my weirdness and our weirdness that held us all together.

I have always been proud to be queer. And I have always prided my QTPOC family for being loudly queer and weird in the face of racist and heteronormative expectations for how we must function as queer people. Queerness introduced me to a very specific politic around owning whatever it is about us that incites the violence against us. It took me a very long time but I figured it out; it definitely wasn't just about how we have sex (and not all of us do), it wasn't just about how we formed chosen family or relationships, and it wasn't just about how we are tragically alienated, pushed out and abandoned (because not all of us are).

Queerness is about carving out space in this world to have what we need, to be who we want and desire, and to hopefully, one day, be free.

My vision for the QTPOC future has evolved and shifted over the years and what I consider as "being free" has changed significantly. With those I love, with those who are my kin, we have envisioned many kinds of possibilities, realities, and futures. We work, strive, and fight for the possibility of a QTPOC future every single day. And, like most things, we pride ourselves in the daily work of liberation.

What has been challenging as we talk about the daily work of liberation is the hesitation to think about disability and queerness simultaneously. Nowadays, I have a lot of folks I can look to, fellow sick and disabled queers of color who know that the way to liberation requires us to engage with ableism when many of those we are closest to aren't ready or even willing to talk about it. But still, in most dominant spaces, even the ones that are proclaimed to be radical, revolutionary, and intersectional, the obvious and transformative relationship between disability justice and queer liberation is silenced.

I have found that in a lot of spaces when we talk about queers loving each other, caring for each other, and witnessing each other intimately, sexually, and otherwise in non-normative ways, we do not consider disability. We do not think to create and hold space for disabled queers of color.

There are reasons for this. One being that ableism traps us in this capitalist system that prioritizes bodies that are able to produce and function in ways that translate into profit. Another being the reluctance in communities of color to say that we are sick or in pain or disabled. When the world around us already challenges our ability to survive, we see it as our responsibility to make sure we don't claim any other barriers; that even when we can't do something we will do it anyways because signs of our weakness are more profitable to systems of dominance than they are to us. But distancing ourselves from that identity and experience reinforces the stigma around disability.

Many of us have been able to transform and reclaim queer-ness so that it is not a weakness. But we have not worked at intentionally unlearning the ideology that makes disability weak. We have not put in the work to unapologetically tell the sick and disabled queers in our lives that it's weird to be disabled, it's okay to be disabled, it's fucking great to be disabled. And in that lack of intent, in that disregard, we leave behind the sick and disabled queers of color who should be rightfully leading the way.

Sometimes it's confusing to me, and even upsetting and heartbreaking, that we forget and leave behind disabled queers of color. Because, like queerness, when I think about disability, one of the first things that comes to my mind is the system that forces normalization on our bodies. And ableism, in particular, seeks to dehumanize and harm disabled people. For me there is a commonality that exists for queers and disabled folks: there is no body that exists that is truly fit for this ableist and capitalist system. There is no body that exists (and not due to ableism alone) that is fit, on a human level, to be perfect or enough. I don't say this to minimize the depth in which ableism directly affects the lives of disabled folks; I don't say this to say that what a non-disabled person experiences is the same as me.

But what I do think is important to acknowledge is that none of our bodies are enough within the state or systems of oppression. Disabled bodies, queer bodies, fat bodies, bodies of color, femme and feminized bodies face the violent forces that desire us to be able-bodied, heterosexual, skinny, white, and masculine.

With this common thread of forced normalization you'd think it would make sense to push ourselves to build for a queer liberation that also means disability justice. And I know that many of us who fight for disability justice, who talk about it daily, who dream of it daily don't do it divorced from queer liberation.

When we think of a QTPOC future we need to make sure to make ourselves grow, revel, and learn with the understanding that ableism and its mechanisms for determining which bodies are worthy and unworthy permeate all of our lives, whether we are disabled are not.

Queers need to act with disability justice in mind; when we demand to resist the neo-liberal grip on our lives, when we fight to reject assimilationist agendas, we need to remember that disability justice is about that resistance and rejection. Above all, it is about redefining what is normal. Disability justice pushes us all to confront the dominant systems that want us to remain entrenched in individualism and in capitalism. Ableism and heterosexism both seek to keep us away from building with each other, caring for each other, and looking out for each other. Both deny us the freedom to define our own bodies, relationships, and desires.

Disability justice not only has deep parallels with queer visions and dreams, it is itself undeniably necessary to queer visions and dreams. Disability justice is so very queer.

When queers talk about being weird, we have to also mean the weird we don't experience. When queers talk about being freaky, we have to also mean the freaky that our spaces often alienate. When queers talk about liberation, we have to also mean liberation for those of us who are disabled.

The QTPOC future that I want rejects what bodies are considered normal and worthy and values, uplifts, and cherishes the bodies that are abnormal and freaky. And in that, prioritizes the intersections of experience, the overlapping desires to be free from trauma, alienation, and isolation. I want a QTPOC future that embraces the interlocking visions for more possibilities of how we can all be and become.

We have been all preparing for the apocalyptic, explosive and revolutionary moment. And I am looking forward to the morning where QTPOC build a new, better world. I am certain that disabled QTPOC will survive. So be certain too and be pre-pared for us.

Ngọc Loan Trần *is a Viet/mixed-race disabled queer writer grounded in the U.S. South. Their work is about bold, fearless visioning that cuts through the nonsense to make real the free-dom, justice and love we seek. You can read more of their work and writing at nloantran.com.*

Works Cited

Mariame Kaba/No Selves to Defend: A Legacy of Criminalizing Women of Color for Self Defense. Prison Culture, 2014

Abbott, Frederick H. The Administration of Indian Affairs in Canada. Washington DC: Board of
Indian Commissioners, 1915.

Dewar, Jonathan. Alex Janvier: Reflections (remarks and Interview). Reconcile This! West Coast
Line 74 vol 46 no 2,Summer 2012 Copyright 2012.

Extian-Babiuk, Tamara. "To Be Sold: A Negro Wench" Slave Ads of the Montreal Gazette 1785
-1805. McGill University Masters Defense, 2006.

Nelson, Charmaine. From African to Creole: Examining Creolization through the Art and
Fugitive Slave Advertisements of Eighteenth- and Nineteenth-Century Canada and Jamaica.

Tuck, Eve and K. W. Yang. "Decolonization is Not a Metaphor." 2012

Winks, Robin W. The Blacks in Canada, A History. Mc-gill-Queen's University Press, 1997. P.17.

Donovan, Kenneth Joseph. "Slaves in Ile Royale, 1713-1758."
French Colonial History 5, no. 1
(2004): 25-42. doi:10.1353/fch.2004.0004.